Discount Airfares

The Insiders' Guide

Second Edition

How to Save up to 75% on Airline Tickets

Priceless Publications

George E. Hobart

Discount Airfares—The Insiders' Guide

How to Save up to 75% on Airline Tickets

George E. Hobart

Copyright © 1998
All Rights Reserved
Priceless Publications
P.O. Box 411
Quilcene, WA 98376

Printed in the United States of America
Book cover design by De Lynn Hobart

Second Edition- January 2000

Hobart, George E.
Discount Airfares — The Insiders' Guide
How to Save up to 75% on Airline Tickets

ISBN   0-9665728-1-5
Library of Congress Catalog Card Number: 99-98083

Published By:
Priceless Publications
P.O. Box 411
Quilcene, WA 98376

With love and affection

to my daughter, Leah

ACKNOWLEDGMENTS

The author would like to thank Beth Nelson, Claudia Nelson, Shirley Canterbury, Tim French, and Leah Hobart for their typing and proofreading assistance. Without their help this project would never have reached completion.

DISCLAIMER

This book was written for educational purposes only, and is sold with the understanding that neither the author nor Priceless Publications assume any liability for loss, damage (direct or indirect), or inconvenience caused by the use of this information. Although great effort has been made to make this source book as complete and accurate as possible, there may be mistakes. No payment has been received by any firm listed herein and any errors, omissions, or inaccuracies are unintentional The book is meant to serve only as a general guide. The author is not engaged in providing legal or professional services. The assistance of a professional should be obtained if that help is required. You may return this book for a full refund if you do not want to be constrained by the above conditions.

If Airlines Sold Paint

Customer: Hi, how much is your paint?

Clerk: Well, sir, that all depends.

Customer: Depends on what?

Clerk: Actually, a lot of things.

Customer: How about giving me an average price?

Clerk: Wow, that's too hard a question. The lowest price is $9 a gallon, and we have 150 different prices up to $200 a gallon.

Customer: What's the difference in the paint?

Clerk: Oh, there isn't any difference; it's all the same paint.

Customer: Well, then, I'd like some of that $9 paint.

Clerk: Well, first I need to ask you a few questions. When do you intend to use it?

Customer: I want to paint tomorrow, on my day off.

Clerk: Sir, the paint for tomorrow is the $200 paint.

Customer: What? When would I have to paint in order to get the $9 version?

Clerk: That would be in three weeks, but you will also have to agree to start painting before Friday of that week and continue painting until at least Sunday.

Customer: You've got to be kidding!

Clerk: Sir, we don't kid around here. Of course, I'll have to check to see if we have any of that paint available before I can sell it to you.

Customer: What do you mean check to see if you can sell it to me? You have shelves full of that stuff; I can see it right there.

Clerk: Just because you can see it doesn't mean that we have it. It may be the same paint, but we sell only a certain number of gallons on any given weekend. Oh, and by the way, the price just went to $12.

Customer: You mean the price went up while we were talking?

Clerk: Yes, sir. You see, we change prices and rules thousands of times a day, and since you haven't actually walked out of the store with your paint yet, we just decided to change. Unless you want the same thing to happen again, I would suggest that you get on with your purchase. How many gallons do you want?

Customer: I don't know exactly. Maybe five gallons. Maybe I should buy six gallons just to make sure I have enough.

Clerk: Oh, no, sir, you can't do that. If you buy the paint and then don't use it, you will be liable for penalties and possible confiscation of the paint you already have.

Customer: What?

Clerk: That's right. We can sell you enough paint to do your kitchen, bathroom, hall and north bedroom, but if you stop painting before you do the bedroom, you will be in violation of our tariffs.

Customer: But what does it matter to you whether I use all the paint? I already paid you for it!

Clerk: Sir, there's no point in getting upset; that's just the way it is. We make plans based upon the idea that you will use all the paint, and when you don't, it just causes us all sorts of problems.

Customer: This is crazy! I suppose something terrible will happen if I don't keep painting until after Saturday night!

Clerk: Yes, sir, it will.

Customer: Well, that does it! I'm going somewhere else to buy my paint.

Clerk: That won't do you any good, sir. We all have the same rules. Thanks for painting with our airline.

An anonymous article from the Internet recently reprinted in Travel Weekly.

Forward

George Hobart has created an incredibly useful tool—*Discount Airfares—The Insiders' Guide,* and in the second edition made it even better. The author has updated his sources, rewritten some chapters, and expanded others. He's also made the book easier to use and, wherever possible, has utilized Internet addresses to assist in research. There is, in fact, an entire section which has been completely revamped and is devoted to the Internet.

The book also has new sections devoted to Students and Seniors that are chock-full of money saving tips. Some of George's advice will surely make the carriers cringe, but there's nothing illegal, and besides, his allegiance is to the traveling public—not the airlines' stockholders.

In addition to updated facts and figures, the book is now much easier to use. For example, the chapter on Consolidators contains a number of fare tables that help consumers research the purchase of the least expensive airfare from Seattle to London. By using this as a case in point, the author walks you step-by-step through an otherwise Byzantine process of finding the cheapest place to buy your ticket.

One thing that everyone can agree upon about Mr. Hobart is that he's one pragmatic fellow. That's very good news for those of us who like to save money.

Robert F. Kay

(Robert Kay has written guide books to the South Pacific published by Lonely Planet and Ulysses Press. He is also the author of Fijiguide.com, the Internet's leading web site on the Fiji Islands.)

Contents

PART III

APPENDIXES

INDEX

Preface

■ AIRFARE CONFUSION

Today it is all but impossible for the average traveler to stay on top of all the complex airline fare changes. Even travel agents are unable to keep up with the hundreds of changes that are made every day. We are constantly hearing about flight bargains, but lack the ability to seek these prices out for ourselves. We simply lack the knowledge, or information, to remedy this situation. What can the average part-time traveler do to avoid this "ripped-off" feeling? Well, you've taken the first step. Read on.

■ BEGINNINGS

Recently I was having lunch with a group of my colleagues, when we began talking about upcoming vacation plans. I work as an elementary schoolteacher, and we were approaching our annual Christmas vacation. All the teachers had plans. One teacher had plans for a trip to La Paz, Mexico; another was anticipating a Caribbean Cruise. In the course of our conversation, we discussed the costs of our planned excursions. The major expenditure in all of the preparations was the cost of the airfare.

Anyone who has taken an airline flight in the past few years, realizes that prices are "all over the board." One person will pay twice the price of another for tickets to the same destination. During our lunchroom discussion, we realized that none of us had the expertise to purchase tickets consistently at bargain prices. Occasionally we were able to acquire bargain tickets on our own, or through the services of a travel agent. However, for the most part, we simply accepted the rates we were quoted and bought our tickets.

As a schoolteacher, I have the ability to go on short vacations several times each year, if I can afford the price of getting there. We have two weeks at Christmas, one week in the spring, and two months during the summer. If I could only afford the airfare, I would love to travel. This situation got me thinking.

I began to investigate the situation in order to become a knowledgeable consumer. The information was very difficult to obtain. I located a few difficult- to- find articles on "flying cheap" or "low cost airfare," but little information was available on the subject. I decided to change that situation and make the information obtainable to the general public. This book is the result of that quest.

■ INITIAL CONSIDERATIONS

To understand the basic strategies that you can utilize to obtain the lowest ticket prices on airline flights, you must have some fundamental understanding of the way airlines make their money. On any given flight, the people seated across a row of airline seats pay fares that vary up to 50%. Business travelers and full-fare coach passengers assure the airline their profit on these flights. However, about 20% of these seats are filled by passengers paying substantially less than full-fare. What is their secret? Their secret, and the underlying principles of this book, is knowledge and flexibility. This book can give you the knowledge. The flexibility is something you have to develop on your own.

What exactly do I mean by flexibility? Well, flexibility begins by not over-planning your trip in the initial stages. To improve your opportunity to save money on airline fares, your trip should be planned as follows:

- **Destination**. A geographical area.
- **Time.** A season rather than a month. Travel on a weekday and avoid weekends on international flights. The same is usually true for domestic flights, but some airlines offer cheaper fares for weekend flights. Time of day can also be a consideration. Often, red-eye (early morning), flights, will be at a reduced fare.
- **Airline.** This should be the last decision and should be based on fare comparisons. If you have the ability to loosely plan your trip in this fashion, you have the potential to make huge savings on the fare you will pay. This is what I mean by flexibility. I realize business travelers will find it much more difficult to incorporate this flexibility into their plans, but with a little pre-planning

many of these options can be incorporated into your plans. It might require a little more creativity to accomplish, but it can be done.

■ THE PLAN

This book gives you the knowledge necessary to get the most for your airfare dollars. Some of the techniques are probably familiar to you and are easy to employ. Others require a bit more effort and imagination. Some of the strategies or techniques can be combined to create additional savings. The only factor limiting their use is your imagination and inventiveness. The approach you use will depend upon your personal taste.

■ A LOOK AHEAD

Before beginning an examination of the strategies necessary to obtain the greatest value for your airfare dollars, let's take a look ahead at how to make the best use of the information you will find on the following pages.

Part I of the book explains the seven most commonly used strategies to obtain bargain airfares. Let's look at an example using a round-trip ticket from Seattle, WA to London, UK.

Seattle, WA ... London, UK.

First Class	$4,507
Business Class	$3,024
Coach	$1,830
Coach (cheapest w/internet search)	$905
Apex (promotional w/restrictions)	$473
Charter	$300-$499
Consolidator (seasonal)	$300-$750
*Courier (leaves from New York)	$150-$200

* This fare will require the additional cost of a low fare or upstart airline ticket from Seattle to New York. Later in this book you will learn how to obtain this fare for between $99 and $199.

The book is divided into three parts. Part I, the seven basic strategies, explores the seven most common, and easiest to use methods to purchase bargain airfares. Included in this section is the use of ticket consolidators, charter flights, air courier services, air passes, advance purchase excursion tickets, online resources, and the use of new or upstart airlines. These are the most common, most conservative, and easiest to use methods of purchasing discount airline tickets.

Part II of the book, Specialized Tactics, presents 15 additional specialized strategies that can be employed to save you money (and sometimes a great deal of money) on your airline tickets. These methods are esoteric, and are probably not familiar to most people. Many of these not-so-common tactics can help you obtain additional savings that can range from 25-80%. The fact that most people are probably unfamiliar with a method will work to your advantage. If everyone were employing these methods, the airlines would soon find a way to prohibit their use. Many of these approaches can be combined to obtain even greater savings. This section of the book will provide many ideas for those with adventurous spirits.

Part III of the book presents an additional 15 "Short Subjects." These simple strategies can often be combined to gain even greater savings. Often these techniques can be piggybacked with your basic strategies creating enormous savings.

PART I

Seven Basic Strategies

Apex

Consolidators

Charter Flights

Air Courier

Air Passes

Online Resources

Upstart Airlines

Apex

The Advance Purchase Excursion Fare (APEX) is really a promotional fare, but it will be discussed separately since it is so common. While apex, in its strictest sense, only applies to promotional fares on international flights, the public has begun to use the acronym for any advance purchase ticket which provides substantial savings over full-fare.

The airlines have given their domestic programs names such as, Easy Saver, Super Saver, etc. These promotional fares are often 15-75% off the cost of full-fare. If your vacation or travel plans can be made months ahead, an apex fare should be considered if it is available.

Only a certain number of seats are made available for these promotional fares and they come with a number of restrictions. The typical promotional fare will carry restrictions that say the ticket must be purchased 7 to 30 days in advance of departure. Generally, only round-trip tickets are made available, and there is usually a substantial fee to make ticket changes in case your plans change. These tickets are usually non-refundable and the travel must all take place between specific dates spelled out on the ticket.

The airlines language usually states that "conditions are subject to change without notice," and that "additional restrictions may apply." In addition, there are some additional fees of $25-$50 which are generally not included in the quoted price of the fare.

For the part-time traveler who is planning well in advance, and expects no changes in their itinerary, apex fares are often among the lowest available.

Here are some examples of some typical peak season apex round-trip fares:

	Peak Season	No Restrictions
Sea/Mia	$295	$1,377
Sea/London	$595	$1,819
N.Y./London	$525	$1,400
N.Y./Mia	$176	$1,320
L.A./N.Y.	$296	$1,844

Consolidators

The average airline only fills about 75% of its seats through normal sales. This means they need to sell 25% of their seats elsewhere. Any price for an empty seat is better than a "no sale." Unsold seats represent an expense (moving empty seats around the world), and with the competition in the airline business, expenses must be cut. Enter the flight consolidator:

■ WHAT ARE AIRLINE CONSOLIDATORS ?

In recent years there has been an explosion of airfare wars and airline bankruptcies. There is increased pressure on the airlines to sell all of their available seats. An airline consolidator provides the airlines with the opportunity to "sell out" seats on their schedule which they were unable to accomplish through their normal outlets. Buying a ticket through a consolidator can often save the knowledgeable traveler 10-40% off published fares.

A consolidator is an airline ticket wholesaler. The consolidator obtains unsold tickets below published fares from an airline, adds a commission, and resells the tickets. A substantial amount of the consolidators' savings is passed along to the ticket purchaser. The airline, of course, is not about to publicize this situation, and asks the consolidator to be "low key" and not use the airline's name in advertising these bargain fares. As competition among the airlines has increased, more and more of these "bucket-shops" — a term initially given to the numerous consolidators in London (on Earls Court Road)— have sprung up around the international hubs such as New York and San Francisco.

There are several different types of consolidators. There are consolidators who specialize in tickets to, or from, certain specific locations. Some specialize only in selling to travel agents, and others concentrate on selling directly to the public. The part-time traveler needs to become aware of, and include, these consolidators in their travel plans. Use of these consolidators can save the traveler 10-40% off published fares. The greatest savings are usually on International fares. However, huge savings are also available on domestic flights. While both economy and first-class tickets are available from the consolidator, the savings are usually greater on coach class.

■ CAN I TRUST A CONSOLIDATOR?

Given all the advantages of booking through a flight consolidator, your question should be, "Why doesn't everyone use one?" Well, as with everything in life, there can be drawbacks. The potential for savings has to be balanced against the possibility of a problem.

If you decide to work through a flight consolidator, you will quickly learn that they do not provide the same level of service as travel agents. Their business is selling airline tickets, not helping you plan a trip. If you are looking to have all of the work done for you, select a good travel agent. The flight consolidator is for the energetic, flexible, independent traveler.

In the past few years, airline consolidators have had their reputations tarnished by a series of bankruptcies. We have all heard stories of travelers stranded in some foreign city unable to return home. While the possibility of being cheated by an unscrupulous or unreliable consolidator is small, it is a risk the wary traveler is always alert to avoid. In a later section of this book, a series of tips will be presented to help you avoid contact with these disreputable salesmen. However, as with any other business transaction, the rule must always be, "Let the buyer beware." The best way to beware is to be knowledgeable.

■ HOW SHOULD I SELECT A CONSOLIDATOR?

How do you go about selecting any product you are about to purchase for several hundred dollars? Begin by shopping around to find the best price for a comparable product. The second step is to check out the dealer or seller of the product.

As you begin to shop around, you will notice that the fares for a particular destination vary between every "shop" you call. Make sure you are shopping for comparable products. Does the quoted price include all fees and any applicable taxes? Will you receive frequent flyer mileage with your purchase? Are you flying on a regularly scheduled airline or as a passenger on a charter flight?

Are your tickets non-refundable or non-transferable in the event your flight is delayed or canceled? What are the charges to cancel or upgrade your ticket? How soon will you receive your tickets after payment?

No discussion of selecting a consolidator would be complete without an answer to the question; "May I use a credit card to make the purchase?" *ALWAYS* use a credit card to purchase your tickets. In the unlikely case of a problem, you have the backup as assistance (and a possible refund) from your credit card company.

After you are satisfied that you have selected the best price for the product, it is time to move to step two. Now it is time to check out the reputation of your consolidator. There are several ways to accomplish this task. If you live near the physical location you can drive by and check their offices. If this is not possible, you can always call the Better Business Bureau in their vicinity and ask if they have received any complaints about the company. In addition, it never hurts to ask how long they have been in business.

This would be a good time to visit your local library or bookstore. Locate the travel section. Find some books about travel to your destination and see if you can locate a list of consolidator references. In the travel section locate a *Fodor* or *Frommer* guidebook and check their recommendations. Usually, they only list consolidators with good reputations who have been in the travel business for a number of years. Just because you cannot find a recommendation does not mean the company is unreliable, but it is a decision ultimately left to the consumer.

Here are some typical consolidator's round-trip fares:

	Peak Season	Low Season	No Restrictions
N.Y./Sea	$285	$249	$1,780
Sea/London	$639	$498	$1,819
L.A./N.Y.	$296	$199	$1,844
L.A./London	$713	$481	$1,875
L.A./Hong Kong	$795	$648	$1,936
N.Y./London	$548	$265	$1,400
Mia/ London	$674	$427	$1,185
Chi/ London	$702	$357	$1,689

■ SAMPLE FARE SEARCHES

OK, before we look over the list of consolidators, we need some basic information. I will try to get a bargain on a round-trip ticket from Seattle, WA to London, England. I have selected some specific dates several weeks in the future (summer 1999).

Here is an example of how I would use the following consolidator list to locate a discount airfare. In example A (Seattle to London), My first step is to call the airlines and get some quotes on the fare.

Example A	Seattle to London	
Canadian Airlines	lowest coach fare	$1262
United Airlines	lowest coach fare	$1113
Northwest Airlines	lowest coach fare	$882
American Airlines	lowest coach fare	$882

It looks like the best I can do purchasing directly from the airlines is $882.

Now I call a local travel agent and check their price for the fare.

Travel Agent	lowest coach fare	$877

Now I know that the basic fare is about $880. This is the fare I hope to beat in order to feel like I have found a true bargain.

Let me make some suggestions on possible ways to use the following list for those of you who have never dealt directly with a consolidator. I would start with my destination. Check the list and find some companies that specialize in that destination. Here's who I picked to call.

Air 4 Less	lowest coach fare	$842
Mr. Cheaps	lowest coach fare	$759
All Continents	lowest coach fare	$599
EZ Travel	lowest coach fare	$590
Travel Team	lowest coach fare	$550

Now for a few online searches.

www.newfrontiers.com	--------------------------	$565
www.tiss.com	--------------------------------	$583
www.a-travel.com	---------------------------	$587
www.flifo.com	--------------------------------	$595

www.economytravel.com ---------------------- $608
www.counciltravel.com ------------------------ $631
www.interworldtravel.com --------------------- $640
www.aesu.com -------------------------------- $667
www.airfarestore.com ------------------------- $695
http://www.airfare.com------------------------ $756
www.traveldiscounts.com ---------------------- $767

I started with a fare of $880 and have now found a discount ticket for $550. I have just saved $330 on each ticket I am about to buy. That's about a 40% saving on each ticket. Is this the best possible bargain for this trip? Maybe not.

Later chapters in this book will explain how to book a courier flight ($300-$600 for this itinerary). I have seen E-Fares (special Internet fares that must be purchased online) of $309 for this city pair, but that was in "Low Season" and I doubt that any real specials are available for the summer. Still, in order to be sure, I check the airline Internet sites to be sure (learn more about how to access this information in the chapter entitled Online Resources).

If you have read through the book, you know from the Flexible Flyer chapter that it is possible to go to Europe from Seattle for $478 anytime of year. That chapter also explains the special conditions associated with that travel. All things considered, $550 seems to be the bargain I was seeking. Here are two more examples of possible searches; (I left out the actual fares because the method is the essential element).

If you are looking for a domestic airline ticket, select about a half dozen companies specializing in those tickets. Give them a call and check their fares.

Example B   Domestic Transcontinental Flight

Bloodhound Travel
Cheap Tickets
Discount Travel Int'l
800-Fly-Cheap
Gary Marcus Travel
Service Travel

At this point if I have a computer, I would do a few Web site consolidator searches. To locate the URL of consolidator Web sites, pick from the list at the end of this chapter. Since it is difficult to know which consolidators have arrangements with which airlines, simply try a few and see if you get a good quote. After a little experience, you will determine the sites you are most comfortable using, and those favorites are the ones you will return to time after time.

www.flifo.com
www.air-fare.com
www.lowestfare.com

By now, I think I have a good idea what price would be a bargain for this trip. Now I'm ready for a telephone or online purchase.

Example C   International Flight to India

Asia Travel Services
ATC Inc.
General Tours
Hari World Travels, Inc.
MT&T
New Wave Travel
Festival of Asia

Now for a few online searches.

www.1travel.com
www.flifo.com

I am not recommending any of these companies, but simply taking them from the list at random. Call and check the fare. You are likely to see a wide range of prices. If you are not satisfied, call six more. Eventually you will feel you have a handle on a discount rate to your destination.

Keep in mind that a thorough search for a consolidator will usually involve checking the Sunday travel section of a metropolitan newspaper as well as surfing through several Internet consolidator Web sites to get some inkling about a true bargain.

Here is a comprehensive list of consolidators who sell directly to the public. Appendix A lists consolidators that sell only to travel agents.

COMPANY	PHONE	SPECIALTIES
800-Fly-Cheap	800-359-2432	US
2M Intl Travels	800-938-4625	Selected Worldwide
Adventure Int'l Travel Service	800-542-2487	Eastern Europe
Aereo (Cut Throat)	800-755-8747	Selected Worldwide
AESU Travel	800-638-7640	Europe
Africa Desk,The	800-284-8796	Europe, Middle East, Africa
Air 4 Less	800-656-9247	Worldwide
Air Brokers Int'l, Inc.	800-883-3273	Around-the-World
Air Travel & Tours	800-938-4625	
Air Travel Discounts	800-888-2621	Europe, Asia
Airbound	415-834-9445	
Airfare Busters	800-776-0481	Worldwide
Airfare Hotline	800-455-2359	Western Europe, Orient
Airkit	213-482-8778	Europe
Airkit	415-362-1106	Europe
Airvalue	903-597-1181	Selected Worldwide
AIT/Anderson Int'l	800-365-1929	Europe, South America, Malaysia, Africa
Alek's Travel	800-929-7768	Europe
All Continents Travel	800-368-6822	Europe, Africa, M. E.

All Destinations	800-228-1510	Caribbean
All Star Travel	408-247-9743	
All Unique Travel	707-648-0237	Europe, Africa, Middle East, Hawaii
All Ways Travel	800-878-0088	Europe, Asia
All World Travel	404-458-3366	
Alpha Travel	800-793-8424	Europe, Africa, Middle East, Hawaii
Alta Tours	800-338-4191	Europe, Latin America
American Int'l Cons.	800-888-5774	Europe, US, Africa
American Tours	800-553-2513	Central & S. America
American Travel	216-781-7181	Eastern Europe
American Travel Associates	800-243-2724	US
Am-Jet Travels	800-414-4147	India, Asia, Middle East
Angio California Travel	408-257-2257	
ANZ Tours	800-735-3861	Australia, New Zealand
Aries Tours & Travel	214-638-7008	
Arnsdorif Travel	407-886-1343	
Asensio Tours & Travel	800-221-7679	Latin America
Asia Specialists	800-969-7427	Asia
Asia Travel Services	808-944-8811	Asia, US
ATC Inc.	800-872-4601	Europe, Asia, Australia India, Africa

Automated Traveler	800-683-6336	Central & South America, Europe
Azure Travel Bureau	800-882-1427	India, Nepal, Tibet
B & A Travel	800-968-7658	
Balkan Holidays	212-573-5530	Selected Worldwide
Balkan USA	800-822-1106	Bulgaria, Romania
Bargain Airfares	800-922-2886	Selected Worldwide
Berkeley	510-848-8634	Selected Worldwide
BET World Travel	800-662-2640	Selected Worldwide
BET World Travel	800-747-1476	Worldwide
Bethany Travel	800-368-3274	Worldwide
Bloodhound Travel	206-623-4359	US, Hawaii, Mexico
Borgsmiller Travels	800-228-0585	Malaysia
Bravo Tours	800-272-8674	Spain
Brazil Tours	800-927-8352	South America
Brazilian Wave Tours	800-682-3315	Brazil
British Network, LTD	800-274-8583	England
Budget Traveler, The	415-331-3700	Europe, Central America
Buenaventura Travel	800-286-8872	
C & C Travel	800-767-2747	Selected Worldwide
C & G Travel	206-523-0103	Asia, US, Europe
Calcos Tours	212-889-9200	South Africa
Campus Travel	800-328-3359	Europe, South Pacific
Canatours	213-223-1111	Asia, US, Europe

Carbone Travel	800-735-8899	South America
Carefree Getaway	800-969-8687	Asia, US, Europe
Cathay Express Travel	206-622-9988	
Cathay Travel	818-571-6727	Orient, Latin America, North America
Cefra Discount Travel	602-948-5055	Selected Worldwide
Cenatours	213-680-1288	Hawaii, Asia, South Pacific
Central Holidays	800-935-5000	
Central Travel Network	214-943-5400	Hawaii, Central & South America
Chartours	800-323-4444	Worldwide
Cheap Seats	800-451-7200	Selected Worldwide
Cheap Tickets	800-377-1000	US
China Travel Service (USA), Inc.	800-899-8618	China, Hong Kong
Chisholm Travel, Inc.	312-263-7900	Orient, South Pacific
City Tours	800-238-2489	Orient, South Pacific, Latin America,
CL Thomson Express Int'l	213-689-0261	Selected Worldwide
Coast Consolidators	714-528-3366	Europe, South Pacific
Consumer Wholesale Travel	800-223-6862	Selected Worldwide
Continental Travel	310-453-8655	Europe, Hawaii
Cosmopolitan Travel	800-548-7206	Europe, South America
Cosmopolitan Travel Service	800-633-4087	Europe, Africa, Middle East, Latin America

Council Charter	800-800-8222	Caribbean, Western Europe, Martinique
Council Travel	800-226-8624	Worldwide, Student Fares
Crown Peters Travel	800-321-1199	Cairo, Istanbul
Custom Travel	800-535-9797	Worldwide
Cut Rate Travel	800-388-0575	Selected Worldwide
CWT Vacations	800-223-6862	Selected Worldwide
Davis	916-752-8548	Selected Worldwide
Democracy Travel	800-536-8728	Around-the-World
Dependable Travel	708-409-1600	
DER Travel Service	800-717-4247	Europe, Africa, Middle East
DERAIR	800-717-4247	Europe, Africa, Middle East
Destinations Unlimited	800-338-7987	Orient
Detours	800-252-8780	Worldwide
DeTravel	800-637-9597	Selected Worldwide
D-FW Tours	800-527-2589	Europe, Orient, Middle East, Latin America
Dial Europe	800-675-5310	Worldwide, First and Business Class travel
Direct Line Travel	800-422-2585	
Discount Tickets	888-382-4327	US
Discount Travel Int'l	212-362-3636	US, Europe
Dollar Saver Travel	913-381-5050	Worldwide

Downunder Direct	800-642-6224	Australia, New Zealand
Eastern European Travel Center	800-304-3050	Eastern Europe
EBM Tours, Inc.	800-234-3888	Orient
Egypt Tours & Travel	800-523-4978	Egypt, Israel
Egypt Tours & Travel	800-523-4978	Egypt, Israel
Egyptian Connection, The	800-334-4477	Israel, Africa, Middle East
Embassy Tours	800-299-5284	Central & South America
Emerson	808-926-0550	Selected Worldwide
Emmett Travel	800-742-1000	Selected Worldwide
Escape Tours	800-252-0775	South America, Central America
EST Int'l Travel	713-974-0521	Worldwide
Euram Tours Inc.	800-848-6789	Selected Worldwide
Euro Asia Express	800-782-9625	Europe, Asia, South Pacific
Euro-Asia, Inc.	602-955-2742	Europe, Asia
Eurogroups	914-682-7456	Europe
Expanding Horizons	800-421-6416	Asia, South Pacific, Australia
Express Discount Travel	619-283-6324	Europe, Asia, South America
EZ Travel	206-524-1977	Worldwide, Las Vegas
Falcon Travel & Tours	800-272-6394	Worldwide
Fana Travels	800-600-3262	India, Middle East

Fantasy Holidays	800-645-2555	Western Europe
Fare Deals	800-878-2929	Selected Worldwide
Fare Deals Ltd.	800-347-7006	Selected Worldwide
Favored Holidays Inc.	800-735-2112	Selected Worldwide
Fellowship Travel	800-446-7667	Worldwide
Fems Travel	800-790-1016	Scandinavia
Festival of Asia	800-533-9953	Asia, Southeast Asia, Indonesia
Flight Coordinators	800-544-3644	
Fly Wise Travel	800-359-4386	Worldwide
Fly-On	808-524-2200	Selected Worldwide
Flytime Tour & Travel	212-760-3737	Europe, Asia, US
Four Seasons Travel	910-292-1887	Europe, Asia, S.America
French Experience, The	212-986-3800	France
Frosch International	800-866-1623	Israel, , Africa
Garden State Travel	201-333-1232	Asia, Manila
Gary Marcus Travel	800-524-0821	Las Vegas, , US, Europe, Caribbean
General Tours	800-221-2216	India, Europe, Africa, Middle East
Gerosa Tours	800-243-7672	Europe, South America
Getaway Travel Int'l, Inc.	800-683-6336	Latin America, Orient, Africa, Middle East
Glavs Travel	800-336-5727	Russia & CIS
Global Access	800-321-7798	Selected Worldwide

Global Adventures Travel	800-989-6017	Worldwide, Round the World
Globe Tours	800-374-8352	
Globe Travel Specialist	800-969-4562	South America, Europe, Asia
Go Voyages	212-481-7500	Europe
Great Destinations	212-832-7212	Selected Worldwide
Group & Leisure Travel	800-874-6608	Worldwide
GTI Travel Consolidators	800-829-8234	Eastern Europe, Orient
Guardian Travel Service	800-741-3050	Europe
H.O.T. Travel	714-541-2700	Selected Worldwide
Hana Travel Inc.	800-962-8044	Orient
Hans World Travel	800-963-4267	
Hari World Travels	800-889-2968	India
High Adventure Travel	800-350-0612	Around-the World Trips
Himalayan Intl. Tours	212-564-5164	India, Tibet
Hobbit Travel	312-693-8200	Selected Worldwide
Holbrook Travel Inc.	800-451-7111	South America, Africa, Costa Rica
Holiday Tours	800-393-1212	South & C. America,
Holiday Travel International	800-775-7111	US, Las Vegas
Homeric Tours, Inc.	800-223-5570	Greece, Portugal, Pacific Rim, Morocco

Hostways Tours	800-327-3207	Selected Worldwide
Hudson Holidays	800-323-6855	Europe
Inclusive Holidays	800-238-2140	Caribbean
Inka's Empire Tours	212-875-0370	Peru, Bolivia
Inter Island Tours	800-245-3434	Latin America, Caribbean
International Discount Travel	800-466-7357	Latin America, Australia, New Zealand
International Travel Exchange	800-727-7830	Europe, Africa, Middle East, US
Intervac	800-992-9629	Selected Worldwide
Interworld Travel	800-468-3796	Africa, Middle East
Intourist	800-556-5305	Russia, China
ITS Tours &Travel	800-533-8688	Europe
Japan Budget Travel	800-843-0273	Japan
Japan Express	213-680-0550	Japan, Asia
Japan Travel Services	800-822-3336	Japan, Asia
Jaya Travel	877-359-5292	Worldwide
JC Tour & Travel	800-239-1232	
Jensen Baron	800-333-2060	Worldwide
Jet Vacations Inc.	800-538-0999	France, England, Italy, Portugal
Jetway Tours	800-421-8771	Europe, Asia, S America
Kambi Travel Intl.	800-220-2192	Europe, Asia, W. Africa
Katy Van Tours	800-808-8747	Europe, Orient, Middle East

Kitt Holidays	800-262-8728	Australia, New Zealand
Kompas Travel	800-233-6422	Europe
Kristensen Int. Travel	800-262-8728	Australia, New Zealand, South Pacific
KTS Services	800-531-6677	Europe
Kutrubes Travel	800-878-8566	Greece, Albania
Landmark Travel Services	800-556-7902	
Latan American Travel	800-252-0775	Central & South America
Le Soieil Tours	800-225-4723	France, Spain
Leisure Resources	800-729-9051	Europe, Africa
Levon Travel	800-445-3866	Europe, Middle East, Armenia
Long Beach	310-208-3551	Selected Worldwide
Lotus Sun Tours	800-568-8764	Europe, Middle East
LT & Travel	800-295-3436	
M & H Travel, Inc.	212-661-7171	Europe, Orient, Middle East, Africa
Magical Holidays	800-228-2208	Africa
Marco Polo	800-831-3108	Asia
Marcus Travel	800-524-0821	Selected Worldwide
Marrakech Tourist Company	800-458-1772	Selected Worldwide
McAbee Travel	800-622-2335	
Mena Tours & Travel	800-937-6362	North & Latin America
Miami Travel Centre	800-788-0072	Selected Worldwide

Midtown Travel Consultants	800-548-8904	Europe, Orient, Latin America, Africa
Mile High Tours	800-777-8687	Las Vegas, Denver, US
Millrun Tours	800-645-5786	Europe, Orient, Middle East, Africa
Mirabel Travel	800-890-4590	Europe, Israel
Moment's Notice	212-486-0500	Worldwide, Las Vegas
Mr. Cheaps Travel	800-672-4327	
MT&T	500-832-2668	Asia, India
National Travel Centre	800-228-6886	Orient
Nefertai Travel	888-616-3337	Europe, Middle East, Mexico
New Europe Holidays	800-642-3874	Europe, Middle East, Asia
New Frontiers	800-366-6387	France
New Wave Travel	800-220-9283	Asia, India, Middle East, Pakistan
NEWS Travel & Tours	800-992-9629	Selected Worldwide
Norelco Voyager	800-489-4629	Worldwide
Nouvelles Frontieres	415-781-4480	Europe
NTC Travel	800-247-3325	Selected Worldwide
O.E. Tours & Travel	800-783-7396	Worldwide
Omniglobe Travel	800-894-9942	Selected Worldwide
Orbis, Polish Travel	800-867-6526	Poland
Orient Express	800-535-6882	Asia

Overseas Express	800-343-4873	Europe, Orient, Latin America, Africa
Overseas Travel	800-783-7196	Europe, Orient, M. East
Oxford Travel	800-425-9958	Asia, South America, Africa
P & F International	800-822-3063	Eastern Europe, South America, Middle East
Pacesetter Travel	800-663-5115	Asia, Australia, Hawaii
Pacific Gateway	800-777-8369	Selected Worldwide
Pacific Holidays	800-355-8025	Asia
Pacifico Creative Services	800-367-8833	Selected Worldwide
Palm Coast Tours & Travel	800-444-1560	Scandinavia, Orient, Latin America
Palmair	800-526-5892	Europe, Africa
Palo Alto	415-325-3888	Selected Worldwide
Pan EXpress Travel, Inc.	212-719-9292	Europe, South America, Caribbean
Panda Travel	800-447-2632	Selected Worldwide
Panorama Travel	800-204-7130	Russia, Eastern Europe
Park South Travel	212-686-5350	Selected Worldwide
Passport Travel Mgmt.	800-950-5864	Asia, South Pacific
Paul Laifer Tours Inc.	800-346-6314	Eastern Europe
Payless Travel	212-573-8980	
Pennsylvania Travel	800-331-0947	Worldwide
Perfect Travel	800-352-5359	Israel

PERS Travel	800-583-0909	Selected Worldwide
Persvoyage	800-455-7377	Europe, Middle East
Pharos Travel	800-999-5511	Middle East
Picasso Travel	800-462-8875	Europe, Africa, Middle East
Piece of Mind Travel	415-864-1995	
Pino Welcome Travel	800-247-6578	Central America, South America
Pinto Basto USA	800-526-8539	Portugal, Latin America
Pleasure Break Vacations	800-777-1566	Europe, Middle East, Asia
Plymouth Travel	800-736-8747	Worldwide
Premier Travel Services	800-545-1910	Selected Worldwide, Africa
Prime Travel	800-344-3962	Europe, Middle East
Queue Travel	800-356-4871	Worldwide
Rahim Tours	800-556-5305	Scandinavia, Russia, China
Rahway Travel	800-526-2786	Eastern Europe, Ukraine
Raj Travels	212-697-4612	India
Rebel Tours	800-227-3235	Selected Worldwide
Regatta Travel	303-751-0666	Worldwide
Riverside Travel	808-521-5645	Worldwide
RMC	800-782-2674	Selected Worldwide
Royal Lane Travel	800-329-2030	Worldwide
Royal Tours	800-643-8744	Middle East

RTC International	312-853-2700	Selected Worldwide
SAF Travel World	800-394-8587	Asia, Vietnam, Philippines
Saga Tours	800-683-4200	Europe, Orient, Middle East
Scan the World	415-325-0876	Europe, Africa, Australia, Around-the-World
Schwaben Int'l	800-457-0009	Worldwide
Senator Travel	800-736-2121	Europe, Africa, Middle East, First and Business
Service Travel	800-519-2582	Europe, US
Sharp Travel Washington	800-969-7427	Orient
Sherman Oaks	818-905-5777	Selected Worldwide
Skybird Tours	810-559-0900	Asia, India, Europe
Skylink Travel	800-247-6659	Europe, Orient, Africa
Skytours	800-246-8687	Europe
Smart Traveler, The	800-448-3338	Worldwide
Sona Travels	800-720-7662	Europe, Middle East, India
South American Fiesta	800-334-3782	Latin America
South Pacific Express Travels	800-321-7739	South Pacific
S. Pacific Holidays	800-940-1712	Fiji
South Star Tours, Inc.	800-654-4468	Latin America
Southern Connections	800-635-3303	Latin America

Southwest Travel Systems	602-255-0234	Worldwide
Spalding Comers Travel	404-441-1164	Europe, India, Asia, Africa
Specialty Tours Int'l USA Inc.	800-421-3913	South Pacific, Europe, Orient
Spector Travel of Boston	800-879-2374	Africa
STA Travel	800-777-0112	Student & Youth
STA/University Travel	215-382-0343	Selected Worldwide
STT Worldwide Travel	800-348-0886	Selected Worldwide
Sudo Tours	212-302-2860	Asia
Sun Destinations	415-398-1313	Worldwide
Sunbeam Travel	800-433-3161	Selected Worldwide
Sunco-Carison Travel	800-989-6017	Around-the-World
Sunline Express Holidays	800-786-5463	Europe, Asia, South America, Hawaii
Sunnyland Tours	800-783-7839	Europe, Baltics, Russia
Sunrise Travel	800-235-3253	Around-the-World, Worldwide
Suntrips	800-786-8747	Europe, Hawaii, Mexico
Super Travel	800-878-7371	Pakistan
Supersonic Travel	800-439-3030	Europe, Asia
Supervalue Vacations	800-879-1218	Selected Worldwide
TAL Tours Inc.	800-825-9399	England, Greece, Middle East

TCI Access Int'l	800-272-7359	Europe, Middle East, Asia
TFI Tours Intl. Ltd.	800-745-8000	Selected Worldwide
Ticketworld/SAF Travel World	800-394-8587	Philippines, Vietnam
TMV Tours	404-256-4809	Asia, India, Africa
Tokyo Travel Services	800-227-2065	Europe, Asia, South America
Tourlite Int'l Inc.	800-272-7600	Turkey, Greece, Costa Rica
Trans Am	703-998-7676	Selected Worldwide
Transoceanic Travel	415-362-0390	Europe, Asia
Transview Travel	800-553-6762	India, Pakistan
Travac Tours & Charters	800-872-8800	Europe, Africa, Middle East
Travel Associates	800-992-7388	Europe, Middle East
Travel Avenue	800-333-3335	Worldwide
Travel Bargains	800-247-3273	Europe, Asia, US
Travel Beyond	800-823-6063	South Africa
Travel Bound	800-456-8656	Europe
Travel Center	800-621-5228	Selected Worldwide
Travel Charter International	800-521-5267	Europe
Travel Core of America	800-992-9396	Europe, South Africa
Travel Design	415-969-2000	
Travel Interlink	800-477-7172	Asia

Travel Network	800-933-5963	Caribbean, Central & South America
Travel People	800-999-9912	Europe, Asia, South America
Travel Planner	800-336-2757	Israel
Travel Team	800-788-0829	Worldwide
Travel Today Int'l	800-660-6669	Worldwide
Travel Ways	800-876-3131	South Africa
Travnet	800-359-6388	Selected Worldwide
Tread Lightly LTD.	800-643-0060	Latin America
Triple C Travel	301-279-7652	Hong Kong, China, Taiwan
TS Travel	818-346-8600	
Tulips Travel	800-882-3383	Europe, Orient
U.S. International	800-759-7373	Greece, Africa, Israel, Egypt
U.S. Int'l Travel	312-404-0990	Worldwide
Uniglobe Americana	504-561-8100	Europe, South America, Central America
Union Express, Inc.	800-258-3330	Worldwide
Unique Travel	800-397-1719	Europe, Asia, South Pacific
United Tours Corp.	800-245-0203	Eastern Europe
Unitravel	800-325-2222	Europe, Asia, Africa, Latin America, North America
Universal Travel	916-442-8747	Pakistan, Arabia, India

Unlimited World Travel	800-322-3557	Eastern Europe, Worldwide
Up & Away Travel	800-275-8001	Selected Worldwide
US Intl Travel & Tours	800-874-0073	Selected Worldwide
Value Holidays	800-558-6850	Worldwide
Value Travel	800-887-5686	Central & South America
Victor Corp/Faresaver	800-800-8891	Eastern Europe
Visions Travel	800-888-5509	Europe, Egypt
Vytis Tours	800-778-9847	Scandinavia, Baltics
W.L.A.	310-394-5126	Selected Worldwide
Way To Go	213-466-1126	Europe, Asia
Way To Go Costa Rica	800-835-1223	Costa Rica
Way-To-Go Travel	415-864-1995	Selected Worldwide
West Allis	414-475-9400	Selected Worldwide
Wholesale Travel Centre	800-553-6762	India, Pakistan
Winggate Travel	913-451-9200	Korea
World Link Travel Network	310-342-1280	
World Trade Tours	800-732-7366	Central & S. America
World Travel	800-886-4988	Europe, Africa, Middle East
Worldvision Travel	800-545-7118	Selected Worldwide
Wright Travel	800-877-3240	Venezuela, Spain, Greece, Portugal

Zig Zag International Travel	800-226-9383	Asia, Africa, Latin America, Orient
Zohny Travel	800-407-7255	Middle East, Asia

Consolidator Web Sites

a-travel	www.a-travel.com
AESU Travel	www.aesu.com
Africa Desk, The	www.africadesk.com
Air Brokers International	www.airbrokers.com
Air Fares for Less	www.air4less.com
Air Travel Discounts	www.airdisc.com
Airfare Busters	www.afbusters.com
Airfare.com	www.airfare.com
Airfare Store	www.airfarestore.com
All Destinations	www.alldestinations.com
Alpha Travel	www.alpha4travel.com
Azure Travel Bureau	www.azuretravel.com
Balkan USA	www.balkanusa.com
Banana Travel	www.bananatravel.com
Borgsmiller Travels	www.mta-tvl.com
Brazil Tours	www.braziltours.com
Budget Travel	www.budgettravel.com
Carbone Travel	www.carbone-travel.com
Carefree Getaway	www.carefree.com
Cheap Tickets, Inc.	www.cheaptickets.com

Council Travel	www.counciltravel.com
Cut Rate Travel	www.cutratetravel.xt.com
DER Travel Services	www.dertravel.com
Destinations Unlimited	www.air-fare.com
DFW Tours	www.dfwtours.com
Discount-Airfares.com	www.discount-airfare.com
Dollar Saver Travel	www.dstravel.com
DownUnder Direct	www.swainaustralia.com
Economy travel	www.economytravel.com
Egypt Tours & Travel	www.egypttours.com
Embassy Tours	www.embassytravel.com
FAREBEATER	www.flifo.com
Fellowship Travel Intl.	www.fellowship.com
Fly Wise Travel	www.checkairfare.com
Frosch Intl. Travel	www.froschtravel.com
Garden State Travel	www.gardenstatetravel.com
Glavs Travel	www.glavs.com
Global Adventures Travel	www.globaladv.com
Global Discount Travel	www.lowestfare.com
Hans World Travel	www.hanstravel.com
Hari World Travel	www.hariworld.com
Holiday TravelIntl.	www.holidaytvl.com
Homeric Tours	www.homerictours.com
High Adventure Travel, Inc.	www.airtreks.com

Himalayan Intl. Tours	www.himalayantours.com
Inka's Empire Tours	www.inkas.com
Interworld Travel	www.interworldtravel.com
Intourist USA	www.intourist.ru
1travel.com	www.1travel.com
Jaya Travel	www.jayatravel.com
Jetset Tours	www.jetsettours.com
Kristensen Intl. Travel	www.kitt-travel.com
Kutrubes Travel	www.kutrubestravel.com
Latin American Travel	latinamericantravel.com
Lavon Travel	www.lavontravel.com
Mena Tours & Travel	www.menatours.com
Nefertai Travel	www.nefertai.com
New Frontiers	www.newfrontiers.com
Online Discount Air Tickets	www.airfare.com
Overseas Express	www.ovex.com
Palmair	palmairinternational.com
Panda Travel	www.pandatravel.com
Priceline.	www.priceline.com
Prime Travel	www.primetravel.com
Scan The World	www.scantheworld.com
Senator Travel	www.senatortravel.com
Skytours Travel	www.skytours.com
STA	www.sta-travel.com

Ticket Planet	www.ticketplanet.com
Tickets Direct	www.ticketsdirect.com
Travel Bargains	www.1800airfare.com
Travel Discounts	www.traveldiscounts.com
TravelHUB	www.travelhub.com
Travel Information System	www.tiss.com
Travel Network	www.travel-network.com
Travel Team	www.travelteam.com

Charters/Tours

Although they are totally different segments of the travel industry, I have decided to combine the discussion of charter flights, tours, and packages, into one chapter. One reason I chose to lump these three together is the fact that they are very often combined in a travel itinerary. Since this is a book discussing bargain airfares, our chief concern is the charter portion of all three. Let me begin with a brief explanation of the three.

Charter flights usually are not regularly scheduled (Jet Express,, and Sun Country are exceptions that fly regularly scheduled charters). They may be handled by an airline or booked by tour companies, private individuals or businesses. Charters are governed by a different set of "carriage rules" than regularly scheduled airlines. Often low cost airlines—Fiesta West, American Trans Air— begin their operation as charters. Later, as they gain name recognition and more aircraft, they advance into regularly scheduled service. Most of this chapter is devoted to a discussion of charter flights.

"Packages" refer to the combination of various elements of a travel itinerary bundled and priced together. Usually, this is the linking of the air and land portions of a trip (flight, hotel, and often transfers). Responsibilities and payment billing for both ground and air portions of a trip are handled by a single entity. Certain elements of the trip can be altered to meet the changing inclinations of the traveler.

Tours, on the other hand, are completely preplanned. Members of the tour group travel together, share the same accommodations, and have all elements of their travel attended to and prearranged. This often involves being escorted by experienced professional tour guides who take care of lodging arrangements, sightseeing, transfers, tips, gratuities and baggage handling.

Before we focus our attention on charter flights, it might be helpful to consider some of the drawbacks (the advantages are obvious) of packages and tours. A package or tour is only as good or reliable as the "packager." These trips are only available to certain destinations and then only at specific times. Bookings are customarily based on double occupancy. Solo travelers must pay a single room supplement. Major packagers include, but are not limited to, tour companies, travel agencies and airline tour divisions. There are almost always cheaper alternatives.

■ CHARTERS

If you have the ability to fit your scheduled trip into a flexible time frame, charter flights are well worth checking into. Charter flights operate under the principle that if all seats are sold for a flight; they can be sold for less.

Although there are a few winter charters to ski areas and popular European cities, most are operating to transport winter weary travelers to sunny locations in Mexico, Hawaii, the Caribbean, and the South Pacific.

Charter flights do not operate on a regular flight schedule, so you must have the ability to meet their departure time. This constraint will very often rule out those part-time travelers who are on leave from a 9-5 job. However, those who work on their own time schedule, or are retired and are seeking a bargain adventure, find it an excellent opportunity.

Since the primary objective behind charter flights is filling all the seats, they usually only operate between highly desirable locations during the peak season. They are usually not available for a one-way fare. As a traveler, I know the inconvenience of standing in long check-in lines to board a plane where every seat is filled. The size of airline seats makes an entirely sold flight a somewhat claustrophobic experience. We all must decide if the savings (and they can be substantial), make it worth the inconvenience. Certainly a few hours of inconvenience on the airplane are worth several hundred dollars.

Enough with all the negatives of charter flight travel. If you are still reading this section, you are ready to hear some of the attractive features of charter travel. Of course, the most attractive feature is the price which can be as much as 50% off a standard fare. One charter feature that is often overlooked is the fact that it may be the only non-stop option to your destination.

Travelers who enjoy traveling Business Class may find charter fares to be 30-50% less than comparable scheduled carriers. Charter flight are always worth checking during peak season when scheduled airlines fares are at their highest.

Another consideration, when flying charter, is the anticipated departure city. Most major airlines are centered near certain "hubs" or central cities that tie all their flight schedules together. New York, Chicago, and San Francisco, among others, are considered central hubs. Nearly all flights of any given airline make stopovers in these hubs to pick up passengers.

If you depart from a non-hub city, you can fly non-stop directly to your destination without the inconvenience of a stopover in a hub city and a change of planes. Anyone who has made one of those stops with its attendant layover to board another plane, knows that this is just another opportunity for something to go wrong with your trip.

It's also a perfect opportunity for your checked luggage to make its way to the opposite side of the globe. This feature, in itself, should be a huge draw for those who have the ability to fit a charter flight into their itinerary.

Charter flights usually have no long, advance-purchase requirements and can be booked until day of departure as long as seats are available. The most popular charters, to the most desirable locations, usually fill well in advance. The wise traveler, who has made his plans well in advance, will get his tickets as quickly as possible. It is usually possible to arrange your purchase through your travel agent for maximum convenience.

Since the airline has no responsibility to back up a ticket sold by a charter or tour operator, it is essential that you select only a reputable operator. We have all heard about the tour operator who goes out of business leaving his patrons stranded at locations around the world. While this is a fairly rare event, it must be considered. The risk can be lessened by checking with passengers who have used the service, and by a call to the Better Business Bureau to check on complaints.

If you live near the airport, it might be possible for you to meet an incoming charter flight in person and ask some of the returning passengers for an evaluation of the tour operator service. "Better safe than sorry."

For some specific information on charter agencies, destinations, and prices, be sure to check the April and November 1998 issues of *Consumer Reports Travel Letter*. Back issues are available. Yearly subscriptions are $39.

Consumer Reports Travel Letter
Subscription Department
P.O. Box 51366
Boulder, CO 80323-1366

It is typically difficult to purchase tickets directly from charter lines, so a good travel agent is usually an integral part of seeking out a reputable charter flight to match your travel plans. Due to the somewhat higher financial risk of direct purchases, my recommendation is to investigate charter destinations and fares, then have a travel agency make the actual purchase.

For those of you who would rather handle all aspects of the transaction personally, here are a few of my favorites that do sell directly to the public:

Canada 3000   www.canada3000.com   888-226-3000
Canada 3000's fleet of Airbus A330-200s, Boeing 757's and Airbus A320s fly to destinations throughout North America, Hawaii, Mexico, and the Caribbean. The airline operates from many U.S. cities and coast to coast in all of Canada's major cities.

Here are some other favorites.

Fantasy Holidays
Rome, Hawaii, California
www.fantasyholidays.com
800-645-2555

Martinair Holland
Amsterdam
www.martinair.com
800-627-8462

New Frontiers
Paris, Tahiti
www.newfrontiers.com
800-366-6387

Pleasure Break
London, Costa Rica
www.pleasurebreak.com
800-777-1566

Sceptre Tours
Ireland
www.sceptretours.com
800-221-0924

Sun Trips
Hawaii, Mexico
www.suntrips.com
800-786-8747

I have compiled a list of the more prominent charter and tour operations and their destinations.

Charter Contacts

COMPANY	PHONE	SPECIALTIES
Aat King's Australian Tours	800-353-4525	Australia, New Zealand, South Pacific
Aberchrombie & Kent Int'l Inc.	800-323-7308	Worldwide
African Travel, Inc.	800-421-8907	Africa, Egypt
All About Tours, Inc.	800-247-8687	Australia, South Pacific New Zealand,
Apple Vacations West	800-727-3400	Mexico, Caribbean, Las Vegas, Hawaii
Apple Vacations East	800-365-2775	Mexico, Caribbean, Las Vegas, Hawaii
Ariel Tours	800-262-1818	Israel
ATS Tours	800-423-2880	Australia, South Pacific, New Zealand,
Australian Pacific Tours	800-290-8687	Australia, Africa New Zealand,
Balair CTA	800-322-5247	Switzerland
Brendan Tours	800-421-8446	Worldwide
Brian Moore Int'l	800-982-2299	Great Britain, Ireland
Celtic Int'l Tours	800-833-4373	Great Britain, Ireland

Central Holidays	800-935-5000	Israel, Africa, Caribbean
Certified Vacations	800-233-7260	Worldwide
CIE Tours Int'l	800-243-8687	Great Britain, Ireland
CIT Tours Inc.	800-248-8687	France, Italy
Classic Custom Vacations	800-221-3949	Greece, Turkey, Italy, US
Club Valtur	800-935-5000	Morocco
Collette Travel Service	800-832-4656	US, South America, Europe, Australia
Contiki Holidays	800-266-8454	Worldwide
Cosmos	800-221-0090	Worldwide
DER Travel Services	800-782-2424	Europe
Discount Travel	212-362-3636	US
Educational Field Studies	800-654-4750	Europe, US
Educational Travel Services	800-929-4387	Europe, Egypt, Israel, Middle East, Australia
Evergreen Holidays	800-443-0070	Ireland
Fantasy Holidays	800-645-2555	Italy
Freegate Tourism	800-223-0304	Europe, Egypt, Israel, Middle East, S. America
Friendly Holidays	800-221-9748	Caribbean, South & Central America, US
Funway Holidays Funjet	800-558-3050	US, Mexico, Caribbean, Europe
Gate 1	800-682-3333	Europe, Africa, Israel, Middle East, Asia
Globus	800-221-0090	Worldwide

Gogo Worldwide Vacations	800-899-2558	Worldwide
Haddon Holidays	800-257-7488	Hawaii
Holland America Line-Westours	800-426-0327	Alaska
Homeric Tours	800-223-5570	Greece, Eastern Europe
Insight Int'l Tours	800-582-8380	Europe, Egypt, Israel, Middle East
Isram World of Travel	800-223-7460	Worldwide
1st Cultural Tours	800-833-2111	Europe Egypt, Israel, US
Japan & Orient Tours, Inc.	800-377-1080	Asia, Australia, New Zealand, South Pacific
Japan Travel Bureau	800-566-5582	Europe
Jetset Tours Inc.	800-453-8738	Hong Kong, Asia, Europe, Australia
Kingdom Tours	800-626-8747	Caribbean, US
Lakeland Tours	800-999-7676	Europe
LTU Int. Airways	800-888-0200	Germany
Mark Travel Corp.	800-558-3050	Europe
Martinair	800-627-8462	Amsterdam
Mayflower Tours	800-323-7604	Caribbean, Europe, Australia, Mexico
MLT Vacations	800-635-1333	Puerto Rico, Mexico, US
New Frontiers	800-366-6387	Paris, Tahiti
Orient Flexi-Pax Tours	800-545-5540	Asia, South Pacific

Pacific Bestour Inc.	800-688-3288	Asia, South Pacific, Australia
Pacific Delight Tours	800-221-7179	Asia
Pleasant Holidays	800-244-9844	Hawaii
Pleasure Break	800-777-1566	London, Costa Rica
Preferred Holidays	800-696-2055	Caribbean, Western Europe, US
Rail Europe	800-438-7245	Europe
Sceptre Charters	800-221-0924	Ireland
Special Expenditures	800-762-0003	Worldwide
Sun Trips	800-786-8747	Hawaii, Mexico
Sunny Land Tours	800-783-7839	Africa, China, Japan, Europe, Middle East
Tauck Tours	800-468-2825	Asia, Europe, US
TBI Tours	800-223-0266	Asia, China, Japan
TNT Vacations	800-262-0123	Western Europe
Trafalgar Tours	800-854-0103	Europe, Israel, Middle East, Central America,
TransGlobal Vacations	800-338-2160	US, Mexico, Caribbean
Trans National Travel	800-262-0123	Mexico, Caribbean
Travcoa	800-992-2003	Africa, Asia, Europe, Middle East, Australia
Travel Bound	800-456-8656	Europe, Middle East
Travel Impressions	800-284-0044	Mexico, Caribbean , US
Vacationland	800-245-0050	Asia, Western Europe, Australia, New Zealand

Vacation Express	800-848-8047	Costa Rica
Way To Go Travel	213-466-1126	Europe, Hawaii
Your Man Tours	800-922-9000	England, US

Tour & Packager Contacts

AAT King's Australian Tours	800-353-4525
Abercrombie & Kent	800-323-7308 www.abercrombiekent.com
Abreu Tours	800-223-1580
Adventure Tours	800-999-9046
African Travel	800-421-8907
Air Jamaica Vacations	800-622-3009 www.airjamaica.com
All About Tours	800-274-8687
America West Vacations	800-356-6611 www.americawest.com
American Tourist	877-687-1000
Apple Vacations	800-727-3400
Asia Trans Pacific	800-825-1680
Asian Pacific Adventures	800-825-1680
Australian Pacific Tours	800-290-8687
Bestour, Inc.	800-688-3288
Brendan Tours	800-421-8446
Brian Moore Int'l	800-982-2299

British Air Tours	800-359-8722
British Airways Holidays	800-247-9297 www.british-airways.com
Capricorn Leisure	800-426-6544
Caribbean Vacations Network	800-423-4095
Celtic Int'l Tours	800-833-4373
Central Holidays	800-935-5000
Certified Vacations	800-233-7260 www.leisureweb.com
CHA Educational Tours	215-923-7060
Char-Tours	800-323-4444
China Focus	800-868-7244
China Vacations	800-868-6686
Christian Tours	800-476-3900
Christian Holidays	800-397-4608
Christian Traveler	800-323-6181
CIE Tours	800-243-8687
CIT Tours	800-248-8687
Classic Custom Vacations	800-221-3949
Cloud Tours	800-223-7880
Club America	800 221 4969 www.clubamericatravel.com
Club Med	800-258-2633 www.vacation-hotline.com
Collette Tours	800-832-4656

Contiki	800-266-8454
Continental Vacations	800-634-5555 www.coolvacations.com
Creative Tours	800-289-8687
Czech Vacations	877-293-4225
Delta Vacations	800-221-6666 www.deltavacations.com
DER Tours	800-937-1235
Discover Wholesale Travel	800-576-7770
Discovery Tours	800-825-0699
Down Under Connections	800-937-7878
Eastern Tours Consolidated	800-339-6967
Educational Tours	800-962-0060
Educational Travel Svcs.	800-929-4387
EF Educational Tours	800-637-8222
Escapes Unlimited	800-243-7227
Europe Express	www.europevacations.com internet only
European Holidays	800-752-9578
Fantasy Tours	800-772-6001
Far West Travel	800-533-1016
Fishing Int'l	800-950-4242
France Vacations	800-332-5332
FreeGate Tourism	www.freegatetours.com

Friendly Holidays	800-221-9748 www.ten-io.com/friendly
Funjet Vacations	800-558-3050 www.funjet.com
Gate 1	800-682-3333
Geo Expeditions	800-351-5041
Gerber Tours, Inc (Student Travel)	800-645-9145 www.gerbertours.com
Global Fitness Advent.	800-488-8747
Global Reach Tours	888-424-6236
Globus & Cosmos	800-221-0090 www.globusandcosmo.com
GoGo Worldwide	800-899-2558
Golden West Tours	800-346-1625
Grandtravel	800-247-7651
Great British Vacations	800-452-8434
Great Escape Tours	800-365-1833
Haddon Holidays	800-257-7488 www.haddon.com
Homeric Tours	800-223-5570 www.homerictours.com
Horizon Tours	888-786-6726
Interisland Tours	800-245-3434
Intervac	800-992-9629
Island Dreams Travel	800-326-6116

Island Vacations	800-367-3450
Islands in the Sun	800-828-6877
Isram	800-223-7460 www.isram.com
IST Cultural Tours	800-833-2111
Jamaican Travel Specialists	800-544-5979
Japan & Orient	800-377-1080 www.jot.com
Jet Vacations	800-538-0999 www.jetvacations.com
JetSet Tours	800-638-3273 www.jetsettours.com/
Kingdom Tours	800-626-8747
KLM/Northwest World	800-470-1111
Magical Holidays	800-223-7452
Mayflower Tours	800-323-7604
Mexico Travel Advisors	800-876-4682
MLT	800-328-0025
Newmans South Pacific Vacations	800-421-3326 www.newmans.com
Orient Flexi-Pax	800-545-5540
Orientours	800-757-1772
Pacha Tours	800-722-4288
Pacific Bestour, Inc.	800-688-3288
Pacific Delight Tours	800-221-7179 www. pacificdelighttours.com

Paul Laifer	800-346-6314
Pleasant Hawaiian Holidays	800-242-9244 www.2hawaii.com
Petrabax Vacations	800-634-1188
Pleasant Tahitian Holidays	800-644-3515
Preferred Holidays	www.prefhol.com
Royal Northwest Holidays	800-818-7799
Runaway Tours	800-622-0723
Sea Air Holidays	800-732-6247
Servitours	800-337-5292
Smar Tours	800-337-7773
Solar Tours	800-388-7652
South American Vacations	800-451-0341
South Pacific Travel Shop	800-894-7722
South Sea Tour and Travel	800-546-7890
Southwest Airlines Fun Pack	800-423-5683 www.iflyswa.com
Special Expeditions	800-762-0003
STA Travel (Student Travel)	800-777-0112 www.statravel.com
Summit Int. Tours	800-527-8664 www.summittours.com
Sun Holidays	800-422-8000
Sunburst Holidays	800-972-9795
Sunmakers	800-841-4321

Sunny Land Tours	800-783-7830 www.sunny-land-tours.com
Sunquest	800-357-2400
Tahiti Legends	800-200-1213 www.tahitilegends.com
Tauck Tours	800-468-2825
Thomas Cook Vacations	www.tch.thomascook.com
Tourcrafters	www.tourcrafters.com
TourScan, Inc.	800-962-2080
Trafalgar Tours	800-854-0103
Transglobal Vacations	800-328-6264 www.tgvacations.com
Travac Tours	www.travac.com
Travcoa	800-992-2003
Travel Bound	800-456-2004
Travel Impressions	800-284-0044
Tropical Bargains	718-837-1657
Tursem Tours	800-223-9169
TWA Getaway Vacations	800-438-2929 www.twa.com/getaway
United Vacations	800-328-6877 www.unitedvacations.com
USAir Vacations	800-455-0123 www.usairwaysvacations.com
VacationLand	800-245-0050
Visit Italy Tours	800-255-3537

World Wide Christian Tours	800-732-7920
Worldwide Holidays	800-327-9854

Major Airline Tour Divisions

Aeromexico Vacations	800-245-8585 www.expomexico.com.mx
Alaska Vacations	800-468-2248 www.alaska-air.com
American Airlines Vacations	800-321-2121 aav3.aavacations.com
Canadian Holidays	800-776-3000 www.cdnair.ca
America West Vacations	800-356-6611 www.americawest.com/vacations
Asian Affair Holidays	800-742-3133
British Air Holidays	800-876-2200 www.british-airways.com
Cathay Pacific Tours	800-762-8181 www.cathay-usa.com
Continental Airlines Vacations	800-634-5555 www.coolvacations.com
Delta Vacations	800-872-7786 www.deltavacations.com
European Vacations	800-223-5500 www.icelandair.is
Fun Pack Vacations	800-423-5683 www.iflyswa.com
KLM/Northwest World Vacations	Must go through travel agent
Milk and Honey Vacations	800-352-5786 www.elal.co.il

Mex Sea Sun	800-531-9321
Midway Vacations	800-996-4392 www.midwayair.com
Qantas Holidays	800-641-8772 www.qantas.com.au
Quick Escapes	800-736-6747 www.renoair.com
SwissPak	800-688-7947 www.swissair.com
TWA Getaway Vacations	800-438-2929 www.twa.com/getaway
United Vacations	800-328-6877 www.unitedvacations.com
USAir Vacations	800-455-0123 www.usairwaysvacations.com
Virgin Atlantic Vacations	800-364-6466 www.fly.virgin.com
World Vacations	800-800-1504 www.nwa.com/vacpkg

Here is some tour information from the chapter on Part-Time Travel Agents concerning educational tour providers. For more information check that chapter.

Educational Tours

CHA Educational Tours
215-923-7060

EF Educational Tours
800-637-8222

Great Escape Tours
800-365-1833

College Tours

AESU Travel
800-638-7640

Gerber Tours, Inc.
800-645-9145

STA Travel
800-777-0112

Air Courier

Of the seven most common methods discussed in Part I, serving as an on-board courier (O.B.C.) presents the part-time traveler the greatest opportunity for savings. The savings realized by serving as a courier range from 40-60%. Imagine the excitement of telling your friends of your travel to several different continents within a year's time. It is possible, and relatively inexpensive, as a courier. It would be a true conversation-starter at any party.

Air courier savings range from about 40% of the standard fare, to the rare reward of a free flight. As you might expect, the opportunity to secure these tremendous bargains carries with it some responsibilities and inconveniences. However, for the flexible adventurer traveling alone, a trip as a courier provides excitement, prestige, and one of the greatest travel bargains available.

Mention traveling as a courier to your friends and they will chuckle and begin talking about hauling a briefcase across the border for some drug kingpin, and being arrested by customs. Possibly they envision a sweating bespectacled, gentlemen in a gray flannel suit with a valise handcuffed to his wrist, carrying valuables to a contact at a distant airport. While these ideas are romantic and thrilling, invoking visions of Humphrey Bogart or George Sanders, they are not representative of today's on-board courier.

For the past 20 years, voyagers worldwide have been traveling at less than half-price as couriers for package-delivery companies. Many small competitors of U.P.S. or Federal Express just don't have the aircraft fleet to compete, so they utilize the public to assist in delivering their packages to cities around the world. By sacrificing your baggage allowance, you too can save 40-60% on international airfares (domestic couriers are not commonly used) by acting as a courier.

■ WHO ARE AIR COURIERS?

Most couriers are just ordinary people taking advantage of extraordinarily low airfares. They are usually traveling alone since they are limited to carry on baggage. The flights they take are almost always round-trips, and the courier company usually dictates their length of stay at their destination. Some companies offer open return dates up to *30* days. Courier flights most often depart from New York, Los Angeles, and San Francisco, although there are flights from other gateway cities such as, Boston, Chicago, Miami, and Vancouver, Canada.

Sometimes the cost of getting to one of these gateway cities wipes out most or all of the savings inherent with courier travel, but often it is possible to combine the use of a consolidator or low-cost upstart as a method to reach an outgoing courier flight. Couriers travel on major airlines that have agreements with the companies employing them.

■ WHAT IS COURIER SERVICE?

As I mentioned earlier, air couriers have been around for a number of years, and for a time they were also employed for domestic flights. Developments that accelerated delivery of domestic packages put an end to domestic courier services, but international service is still going strong. Many companies have found it cost effective to have an individual flyer check their package through customs as luggage, rather than risk the delays possible if it is shipped as cargo.

Shipping companies have found that a courier can take mail and documents through customs quicker than international airports handle their cargo shipments. Cargo shipments usually must be at the airport 5 or 6 hours prior to a given flight, while using a courier allows the company last minute access to a flight.

Cargo shipments are also prone to delays of several hours before delivery to customs. After their arrival at customs, it is not uncommon for them to spend several days before clearing international customs. Customs sometimes holds a cargo shipment for as long as a week before it clears. To add insult to injury, the courier company now has additional storage charges in addition to the cost of transportation.

As you can see, this is an intolerable situation for companies shipping time-sensitive receipts or letters that cannot be faxed. While companies could use their own employees to move these documents, it would be very costly paying for the airfares and losing the employees for several days until return from the delivery. While this may work for delivery of highly sensitive or valuable items (jewelry or diamonds), use of employees or bonded couriers just to fly back and forth is simply too expensive. As a result, we have the marriage with the part-time traveler.

■ BAGGAGE

Although it might be unthinkable for many people to travel to Europe or Asia with just a bag or two of carry-on luggage, traveling as a courier means allowing the company to use your baggage allowance to ship their parcels. View this restriction as a positive factor forcing you to pack sensibly. Most travelers always take more luggage than necessary on their trips, and then are forced to either tote them around a continent or store them in some central location and return later to retrieve them.

Depending upon the airline requirements, you will be limited to one or two bags of certain dimensions to carry aboard the plane. If you have an imagination and are creative, you may have ideas that will allow you to get more items along with you. Couriers have been known to board planes wearing several pairs of pants and shirts, along with a suit coat and heavy overcoat.

It is possible to travel along with a companion and share their baggage allowance (and presumably the ticket savings). Of course there is always the possibility of shipping some items, if they are absolutely necessary. Some airlines have a provision for excess baggage, and for a fee of $25 to $50 will allow you to ship an additional bag.

Learn to pack economically and purchase any truly needed items at your destination. These foreign purchases can always be shipped home after your trip. Probably the best bet is to take essential items in a bag that fits the overhead compartment; carry cameras around your neck, and hand carry a book along with your courier manifest, passport and visa if necessary. A shoulder bag or a large purse is also very useful.

■ WHAT ARE COURIER RESPONSIBILITIES?

In addition to the baggage limitations, there are certain responsibilities expected of a courier. The on-board courier must be over the age of 18, and possess a valid passport. For visa requirements, contact the Consumer Information Center in Pueblo, Colorado, and request the publication, "Foreign Visa Requirements."

Some companies have certain dress expectations, so it is always best to dress professionally: a jacket and tie for men and a pantsuit, dress or any appropriate business attire for women. If you dress casually, but neatly, there should be no problem. Try to avoid cut-offs and unconventional hairstyles.

In addition, some companies have certain expectations about alcohol consumption on or before your flight, so be discrete. It's important to show the company that you are both reliable and professional. Always be on time. Once a company knows you as a reliable veteran, there are often opportunities for special last minute deals, and the "Holy Grail" of the courier — the free flight.

Most often the representative of the courier company will meet you at the airport. The companies usually expect you to arrive about two hours prior to your flight, and often the representative will show just before the flight. The courier companies like to wait as long as possible in order ship last-minute cargo. The representative will quite often go through the boarding process with you until you board. He will give you a one-way ticket, (you will receive the return ticket at the destination airport on your return date), and probably some ID to present to the representative at the other end.

He will also present you with the all-important sealed manifest. Keep the manifest along with your wallet and passport. He may give you a phone number to call upon arrival, although you will probably be met by a representative upon landing at your destination. Make sure you get a phone number in case of a diverted or delayed flight. If English is not commonly spoken at your destination it's always good to know a few key foreign phrases to avoid problems.

Upon arrival at your destination, present your identification to the representative meeting you. If a problem occurs, make sure you have change to call the emergency number. Usually you will clear customs and be out of the airport long before the baggage. Often the baggage is x-rayed and inspected. Custom inspectors realize that you have had no contact with the baggage and that smugglers very seldom use couriers to transport contraband. Since you have had no physical contact with the baggage/cargo, you have no liability. Since you assume no risk or liability, there is no need for you to be bonded. Your only responsibility, now, is to be on time for your return flight, and repeat the process in reverse.

■ HOW AND WHERE DO I CONTACT THE SERVICE?

While all courier companies have different policies, many of their requirements are very similar. Most require that you apply in person, and this can be a problem for those who live far from New York City where many courier companies are based. Many want you to pay in cash rather than with a credit card, and most require a deposit that you will lose if you cancel or miss your return flight. The requirement of a return trip deposit is often waived if you are a veteran with a particular company.

Upon execution of your responsibilities, you can reclaim your deposit. It is up to you to pay the departure taxes (usually $10 to $20), and remember to figure in phone calls and cab fees. If you have used a courier booking service, they usually charge an annual fee of $50. A courier booking service is most economical if you travel several times each year.

The best bet for beginners is to travel to New York City where there are a large number of courier companies and courier booking agents. Courier booking agents offer more destinations than any single courier company since they represent many different courier agencies. Booking agents are also a wise choice for beginners, because they are comfortable with answering questions and giving explanations.

Most courier companies are busy and don't have time to spend going over explanations for a beginner. Be aware that the courier booking agent will charge an extra fee for this extra service. In addition, a courier booking agent can be very helpful in assisting you with special packages or accommodations at your destination, since they are also travel agents.

After completing your arrangements, you will sign a contract and pay the administration fee (the price for your flight). The companies call the rate an administrative fee in order to retain complete ownership of the actual airline ticket. If your flight is canceled, you simply don't get on the next aircraft to your destination. The courier company owns the ticket and you must wait for them to reschedule.

Since the company owns the ticket, you are not technically eligible for the frequent flyer mileage, but don't let this stop you from trying. Always be a member of the airlines frequent flyer program and attempt to get your membership stamped when you board. Often you can locate courier companies and courier booking agents by checking your local phone book. A representative list of courier companies and courier booking agents follows at the end of this section.

■ DESTINATIONS

Courier destinations are constantly changing and are based upon commerce between the cities involved. The route most often used is between New York City and London. Keep in mind that the most popular routes book quickly. In order to take advantage of the savings you must be knowledgeable. Many booking agents provide recorded information you can access before paying their fee. After becoming a veteran, you will probably be able to guess which company is flying to which city, however, initially you will probably do best paying the fee and getting information.

If you have a certain destination in mind and know the courier company flying to that destination, why pay an extra fee to a booking agent? Go directly to the company to make your inquiry. Remember, the first person that pays gets the flight.

Always discuss the length of stay with the company. The length of stay can vary from one day to 30 days, and in some cases it may be variable. Sometimes it is possible to add on other destinations for an additional fee, or to return from a different city. You will never know unless you ask.

Keep in mind most courier companies prefer to be contacted by phone, and many have recorded messages. Long flights such as, New York to Hong Kong or Sidney, Australia, aren't as popular as the European locations, so the companies may employ great discounts in order to encourage people to try these routes.

Courier companies are governed by supply and demand like any other business, so the rules that apply to the airlines apply to them. They are subject to the same demand during peak seasons, so those who travel off-season obtain the best bargains. One country's high season is always another country's low season. When it is a low season to Europe, it is a high season to Australia, so try to take advantage of your knowledge.

Most companies like to book their flights two or three months in advance. As the date of the flight approaches, unbooked flights receive greater discounts. The company has already booked the flight and must have a courier, or they will be forced to cancel or use one of their own employees.

The company may become desperate enough to offer a free flight just in order to get their delivery to its destination. This possibility, or the last minute cancellations of a courier, provides the maximum bargain if you are aware of the possibility. The only way to be aware of these opportunities is to be in touch with the company. If they are aware that you are always available for last-minute services anywhere in the world, you can often have them place you on a list and call you if the opportunity presents itself. These opportunities are usually only available to a veteran courier who is known by the company to be reliable, professional and on-call.

If the company calls with a flight departing in a day or two, don't be bashful about bargaining for a better discount. However, keep in mind they may have 20 other people on their list, so don't be too forceful. You may talk yourself off the list.

Sometimes a courier company has several seats on the same flight. As a hedge against cancellations, sometimes the company may have two seats to the same destination, but on different airlines. Maybe they have flights the same day to nearby cities such as, Paris and Amsterdam. All these are possibilities to be investigated by someone who doesn't wish to travel alone.

■ NETWORKING

Once you become a veteran courier traveler, make sure you are always gaining information. Always ask questions and keep good notes. Ask the representatives you meet about their companies' destinations. Who is the best contact person at their company? Is it possible to get on a list for last-minute deal? If so, how? Don't be overbearing or ask too many questions at a time, but always continue to build your base of knowledge and contacts. Always write all representatives' names in your book. They may be of value later.

You can also learn a great deal by talking to any customs officers who have time to share their insider knowledge with you. Always save names, addresses, contacts, and information. It will mean dollars to you when you travel later. Never miss an opportunity to show the company you traveled with that you are professional and appreciative. A simple thank you note after a flight will go a long way in this direction.

As part of your networking, join any appropriate courier organizations, and send for informational newsletters. All of this should always become part of your informational data compilation. The following should be one of the first to add to your list:

International Association of Air Travel Couriers
International Features
8 South J Street
P.O. Box 1349
Lake Worth, FL 33460
1-407-582-8320

Their current membership fee is $75 and includes a newsletter with the latest up-to-date information. It also includes the ability to fax information for truly up-to-the-minute services.

Worldwide Courier Association
803 West Avenue, Ste 209,
Rochester, NY 14611
Phone: 716-527-0648
Fax: 716-464-9337
1-800-780-4359 ext. 237

Their current fee for a one-year membership is $88, but they often offer a special introductory membership fee of $58.

I am currently a member of The Air Courier Association. They have an excellent bi-monthly publication called *Air Courier Journal*. It is full of valuable information. Use the following information if you wish to contact them.

The Air Courier Association

191 University Blvd.
Suite 300
Denver, CO 80206
Phone 303-279-3600
Fax 303-278-1293
http://www.aircourier.org

- In addition to their publication listing courier flights, prices, and companies to contact, the Association has a number of benefits to its members.
- members preferred hotline
- Medex ID card
- discount hotel directory
- mileage reward certificates
- special airline reports

■ COURIER COMPANIES

The following comparison chart was compiled in 1999, and is for informational purposes only. Destination and rates are constantly changing. Keep in mind these companies are primarily in the freight business (with the exception of the courier booking agencies). For the most part they have little patience answering travel questions. I recommend that if you are interested in courier travel, you become a member of one of the previously mentioned associations.

Here is a list of some selected courier companies and courier booking agents.

Company	Phone	City	St.	Destinations
1 WorldTravel	310-207-6353	LA	CA	Hong Kong
A-1 Int.	305-594-1184	Miami	FL	Caracas
Able Travel & Tours	212-779-8530	NY	NY	London, Paris
Air Cargo Partners	718-529-6814	Jamaica	NY	Worldwide

Air Facility	718-712-1769	Jamaica	NY	S. America
Air Facility	305-418-2035	Miami	FL	S. America
Air-Tech Ltd.	212-219-7000	NY	NY	Worldwide
All Nations Express	718-553-1718	Jamaica	NY	Seoul, Korea
As You Like It Travel	212-216-0644	NY	NY	Worldwide
Courier Network	212-947-3738	NY	NY	Tel Aviv, Israel
Courier Travel Headquarters	708-409-1600	Westchester	IL	London
Discount Travel International	212-362-8113	NY	NY	Europe, S, America, Hong Kong
Discount Travel Int.	305-538-1616	Miami	FL	Same as NY
East-West Express	718-656-6246	Jamaica	NY	Asia, Australia
Excalibur, Int I	310-568-1000	LA	CA	Asia
Film Int.	310-568-8403	LA	CA	
Focus on Travel	800-722-3246	SF	CA	Australia, Asia
Global Delivery Systems	718-995-7300	Jamaica	NY	Europe, Tokyo
Global Delivery Systems	310-670-1823	LA	CA	London
Going Places	305-871-3211	Miami	FL	London, S. America
Halbart Express	305-593-0260	Miami	FL	Europe, Asia

Halbart Express	847-806-1250	G. Village	IL	London
Halbart Express	718-676-8279	Jamaica	NY	Europe, Asia
IBC-Pacific	310-665-1760	LA	CA	Manila, Bangkok
IMS Courier Service	305-771-7545	Fort Lauderdale	FL	Jamaica
International Bonded Courier	310-665-1760	LA	CA	Manila, Seoul, Hong Kong
Int. Bonded Courier	305-591-8080	Miami	FL	B. Aires, Santiago
Johnny Air Cargo	718-397-5099	Wood side	NY	Manila
Johnny Air Cargo	213-386-7080	LA	CA	Manila
Jupiter Air	415-872-0845	SF	CA	Bangkok, Manila
Jupiter Air	310-670-1197	LA	CA	Bangkok, Hong Kong
Jupiter Air.	718-656-6050	Jamaica	NY	London, Hong Kong
Jupiter Air.	847-298-3850	Des Plaines	IL	Bangkok, Hong Kong
Lima Services	305-964-8400	Hollywood	FL	Lima, Peru
Line Haul Services	305-477-0651	Miami	FL	S. America
Marathon Courier Co.	917-740-9971	Far Rock away	NY	London, Hong Kong
Midnight Ex.	310-672-1100	LA	CA	London
Now Courier	310-671-1200	LA	CA	

Now Voyager	212-431-1616	NY	NY	Worldwide
POLO Express	310-410-6827	LA	CA	Australia
POLO Express	415-742-9613	SF	CA	London, Hong Kong
POLO Express	516-371-6864	Jamaica	NY	London
Rush Courier	718-439-9043	Brooklyn	NY	San Juan
Skynet W W	305-477-0996	Miami	FL	
SOS Int.	310-649-6640	LA	CA	Mexico City
Time To Go	305-373-5813	M. Springs	FL	S, America
Trans-Air System	305-592-1771	Miami	FL	Guatemala City, Quito
Travel Courier	718-738-9000	Oxone Park	NY	Europe, S. America
Travel Headquarters	630-620-8080	Lombard	IL	Europe, Hong Kong
UTL Travel	650-583-5074	SF	CA	London, Bangkok
Virgin Express	718-244-7244	Jamaica	NY	London
Way To Go	213-466-1126	LA	CA	Asia, Aust.
World Courier, Inc.	516-354-2600	New Hyde Park	NY	Mexico City, Frankfurt

Air Passes

Air passes should always be a consideration if you plan to do extensive travel inside your foreign destination. Many foreign governments use their national airlines to promote tourism by offering coupons for air travel at reduced rates. These passes or coupon books, allow a certain number of flights within a country, or specified geographic region, at a fixed pre-paid price. Often these prices are low enough to make them competitive with ground or rail transportation. Since time is money, a slightly higher price may balance the competitive edge. If your trip is limited to a few days, time may be a major consideration.

With the exception of certain regional U.S. passes, all air passes must be purchased outside the country you plan to visit. Some passes can be used by anyone inside the country as long as they were purchased outside its borders. Other airlines check to see that only the holder of an international ticket is using the pass. These passes work best for the traveler whose trip is planned well in advance, and intends to do a great deal of traveling within a large country or region.

Each country's programs have their own particular features. Some countries allow you to only purchase the specific number of passes you need, while others specify a minimum and maximum number you can purchase. Some countries do allow unused passes to be returned for a refund, so be sure to check this requirement before making a purchase.

Always check to see if every stopover requires another pass. Let's imagine you are using the Visit Baltic SAS pass. You depart from Oslo on your way to Moscow. Your plane makes a stopover in Stockholm. Does this trip require one pass coupon or two? Another consideration in this case is the fact that SAS requires that your international flight also be on SAS. Since Scandinavia is one of the few countries of the world that do not allow consolidators to sell discount tickets on their airline (SAS), this purchase may not be the bargain it appears at first glance. Always be knowledgeable of the pass requirements.

Air passes are the airline equivalent of the Eurail Pass. They are designed to permit tourists access to large areas of a country or region at a reasonable price. However, unlike the Eurail Pass, they seldom allow unlimited travel inside the country, but rather, allow only a certain number of flights at a bargain price. Often several countries in a region will cooperate to allow travel within their particular region on any one of their airlines.

Below is a selective list of some of the most popular air pass programs. Programs are constantly changing, so call to check any programs well before departure.

Africa

South African Airways
African Explorer
www.saa-usa.com
800-722-9675

- $70-$150 per segment
- minimum of 4/maximum of 8 coupons
- valid 45 days
- South Africa and select African destinations

Air Namibia
Travel Pass
www.airnamibia.com.na
212-290-2591

- $146 for 2/additional coupons $109 ea.
- minimum of 2/maximum of 5 coupons
- valid 45 days
- South Africa and select African destinations

Argentina

Aerolineas Argentinas
Visit Argentina Air Pass
www.aerolineas.com

800-333-0276

- 4 coupon pass $500
- additional 4 coupons $130 ea.
- valid 30 days
- travel within Argentina

Asia

Cathay Pacific
All Asia Pass
www.cathay-usa.com
800-233-2742

- $999 includes fare from U.S. East or Westcoast
- flights include Hong Kong, Tokyo and 14 other cities
- valid 21 days after arrival
- ability to purchase extra time or destinations
- best Asian pass value

SilkAir
Discover Asia Airpass
www.singaporeair.com.au//silkair
800-745-5247

- each flight $119
- no maximum or minimum
- U.S. residents only
- travel to Indonesia, Malaysia, Philippines, Taiwan, Thailand, Cambodia, Burma, and China

Australia

Quantas
Australian Explorer Pass
www.qantas.com
800-227-4500

- 4 coupon pass $554
- additional coupons $146 ea.
- travel within Australia and New Zealand

East/West Airlines of Australia
800-354-7471

- several passes available
- prices vary
- travel within Australia

Ansett Airlines
Visit Australia Pass
www.ansett.com.au
800-366-1300

- 4 coupon pass au $740
- additional coupons au $210 ea.
- travel within Australia
- maximum of 8 coupons
- not available in Japan

Quantas
Boomerang Pass
www.qantas.com
800-227-4500

- $175-$220 per coupon
- minimum of 2/maximum of 10 coupons
- travel within Australia and New Zealand
- valid for length of international ticket

Air New Zealand
G'Day Airpass
www.airnz.co.uk
800-262--1234

- 30 destinations in Australia/27 in New Zealand
- single zone coupons are $62 each
- multi zone coupons are $80 each
- mega zone coupons are $142 each
- minimum of two coupons/maximum of ten

Austria

Austrian Airlines
Air Pass
www.austrianair.com

800-843-0002

- coupons $130 ea.
- minimum of 3/maximum of 8
- European flights on Austrian Airlines, SwissAir, or Crossair
- valid 2 months

Baltic States   **SAS**
Visit Baltic Pass
www.flysas.com
800-221-2350

- 4 coupon pass $370
- minimum of 2/maximum of 4
- travel to Copenhagen, Helsinki, Oslo, Stockholm, Scandinavia, Kiev, Moscow, St. Petersburg and Vilnius
- valid 3 months
- international round-trip from North America on SAS only

Bolivia   **Lloyd Aereo Boliviano Airlines**
Visit Bolivia Pass
www.labairlines.bo.net
800-327-7407

- 4 cities within Bolivia for $200
- each city only once
- international ticket from Miami on Aereo Boliviano

Brazil   **Varig**
Brazil Air Pass
www.varig.com.br
800-468-2744

- 5 coupon pass $490
- 4 coupon pass $350
- travel within Brazil
- no repeating segments

- valid 21 days after 1st flight

Trans Brazil
Visit Brazil Pass
www.transbrasil.com
800-872-3153

- 5 city pass $440
- 2 additional coupons $100 ea.
- valid 21 days after 1st use

VASP
Brazilian Air Pass
www.vasp.com.br
800-732-8277

- 5 coupon pass $450
- additional coupons $100 ea.
- travel within Brazil

Canada

AirBC
Airpass
www.aircanada.ca
800-456-5717

- one week $329/two weeks $439
- travel Western Canada/unlimited standby flights
- flights from Portland or Seattle to Vancouver included
- pass must be purchased in California
- area includes British Columbia, Alberta, Saskatchewan and Manitoba

Caribbean

Liat
Super Caribbean Explorer
www.liat.com
800-253-5011

- 3 stop pass $199
- unlimited stops one direction/one month $357

- no repeat visits

BWIA
Caribbean Airpass
www.bwee.com
800-538-2942

- pass is $399
- flights to 10 destinations in the Caribbean
- valid 30 days

Bahamasair
AirPass
www.bahamasair.com
800-222-4262

- 3 flight pass $250 from Nassau
- 3 flight pass $320 from Miami
- minimum 3 day stay
- various Caribbean destinations

Central America

Aviateca, Lacsa and Taca Air
Mayan Airpass
www.grupotaca.com
800 535-8780
800 225-2272
800-327-9832

- multi-nation Central American pass
- low season passes from $499 to $1259
- some cities excluded

Taca Air
Visit Central America
www.grupotaca.com
800 535-8780
800 225-2272
800-327-9832

- visit a maximum of 8 Central American cities

- minimum stay 3 days/maximum stay 60 days
- priced by destinations

Chile

Lan Chile Airlines
Visit Chile Pass
www.lanchile.com
800-735-5526

- passes range from $300 to $1290
- combined pass $550
- unlimited stops—valid 21 days—no backtracking
- Easter Island can be added for $530

Ladeco Airlines
Visit Chile Pass
www.ladeco.cl
800-825-2332

- unlimited flights within Chile $550
- child fare $330
- valid 21 days
- Easter Island can be included

Colombia

Avianca Airlines
Discover Colombia
www.vip-ve.com/avianca
800-284-2622

- low season/high season specials
- 10 stops in Colombia $224/30 days/all year
- some cities excluded

England

British Midland Airlines
British Midlands Airpass
www.iflybritishmidland.com
800-788-0555

- unlimited flights $109 ea.

- travel in Great Britain and Europe
- valid 90 days
- must be a U.S. resident

British Airways
Air Pass
www.british-airways.com
800-247-9297

- price depends on destinations
- start and finish in London, Birmingham, Manchester, or Glasgow
- cities include Ankara, Berlin, Casablanca, Lyon, Paris, Moscow, Prague, and Stuttgart

<u>Europe</u>

Europe by Air
Multiple European Airlines
www.europeflightpass.com
888-387-2479

- 100 cities in over 20 countries are available
- minimum of 3 coupons/ no maximum
- coupons are $99 ea.
- valid 120 days

British Midland
Discover Europe Airpass
www.iflybritishmidland.com
800-788-0555

- prices vary/$109-$149-2 travel zones
- no minimum purchase
- must be purchased outside Europe
- travel through Europe and U.K.
- travelers age 55 and over get a 25% discount
- best all-Europe pass value

Lufthansa
Discover Europe Pass

www.lufthansa.com
800-645-3880

- first 3 coupons $125 ea.
- additional coupons $105 ea.
- minimum of 3/maximum of 9 coupons
- must be nonresident of Europe
- travel Europe, Middle East and portions of CIS

Iberia
EuroPass
www.iberia.com/ibusa
800-772-4642

- coupons $125 for Europe segments
- minimum of 2/ no maximum for coupons
- valid 90 days
- must be a U.S. citizen
- travel Europe, Middle East, North Africa

British Airways
Europe Air Pass
www.british-airways.com
800-247-9297

- prices vary/$75-$150-4 travel zones
- minimum of 3/maximum of 12 coupons
- valid 7-90 days
- must be a U.S. citizen
- travel Europe, Middle East, North Africa
- includes several airlines

Delta
Visit Europe
www.delta-air.com
800-221-1212

- prices vary/$80-$130
- minimum of 3/maximum of 8 coupons
- valid 60 days

- must purchase in U.S. or Canada
- travel within Europe

Alitalia
Europlus Air Pass
www.alitalia.com/english
800-223-5730

- 3 coupons $300/ additional coupons $100 ea.
- minimum of 3/ no maximum
- valid same as transcontinental ticket
- must purchase in U.S. with Alitalia ticket
- travel within Europe and Middle East

Air France
Euroflyer Pass
www.airfrance.com
800-237-2747

- coupons $120 ea.
- minimum of 3/maximum of 9 coupons
- valid 60 days after 1st use
- one-way flights to 100 European cities
- must purchase pass in U.S.

Northwest/ KLM
Passport to Europe
www.nwa.com
800-374-7747

- 3 flights within Europe $330
- additional coupons can be purchased
- no time limit
- international ticket must be on Northwest or KLM

SAS
Visit Europe Pass
www.sas.se
800-221-2350

- 3 coupons $400/additional coupons $120 ea.
- travel U.K., Europe, and Scandinavia
- travel on SAS or British Midlands Airlines
- valid 90 days
- must have round-trip from North America on SAS

Malev Hungarian Airlines
Hungarian Pass to Europe
See Hungary

Fiji

Air Fiji
Discover Fiji Pass
www.airfiji.net
714-379-8067

- flights within Fiji/three itineraries
- four flights for $236 U.S.
- valid 30 days

Finland

Finnair
Finnair Holiday Ticket
www.finnair.fi
800-950-5000

- 10 coupons $377
- no time limit

France

Air France/Air Inter
La France Pass
www.airfrance.fr
800-237-2747

- basic pass $279
- unlimited travel 7 days in 30 day period
- student or youth pass $189
- valid 1 year
- travel anywhere within France
- must be purchased in U.S.

Hawaii

Hawaiian Airlines
Hawaiian Air Pass
www.hawaiianair.com
800-367-5320

- 5 days $169/7 days $189/10 days $229/14 days $269
- unlimited flights within Hawaii

Aloha Airlines
Island Pass
www.alohaair.com
800-367-5250

- only available to non-residents of Hawaii
- unlimited travel for 7 consecutive days
- 7 day pass is $321

Honduras

Sahsa Honduras
Mayan World Fare
800-327-1225

- minimum 3 cities/maximum 5 cities
- $399
- valid 21 days
- depart from Miami, New Orleans, or Houston

Hungary

Malev Hungarian Airlines
www.malev.hu
800-223-6884

- 3 coupons $300-$380
- flights within Europe on Malev Airlines
- all flights go through Budapest
- additional coupons can be purchased

India

Indian Airlines
Discover India Pass
www.nic.in/indian-airlines

800-223-7776
- unlimited flights $400
- valid 21 days
- no backtracking

Indian Airlines
India Wonder Fares
www.nic.in/indian-airlines
800-223-7776

- 4 flights at $300 ea.
- Unlimited travel for 7 days within regions

Indonesia

Garuda Indonesia
Visit Indonesia Decade Pass
www.aerowista.com/garuda3.
800-342-7832

- 3 flights $300/additional coupons $110 ea.
- flights are within Indonesia
- valid 10-60 days
- maximum of 10 flights/minimum of 3
- segments must be confirmed before leaving us
- flights must begin in Bali, Djakarta or Medan

Ireland

Alitalia
EuroGreensaver Pass
www.aerlingus.ie
800-474-7424

- coupons are $60 for flights within Ireland
- coupons are $69 for flights between Ireland and the UK
- coupons are $99 or flights between Ireland and Europe
- must be purchased in conjunction with Aer Lingus transcontinental ticket
- minimum of 2/maximum of 8 coupons

Italy   **Alitalia**
                                  Visit Italy Pass
                                  800-223-5730
- 3 flight coupons to 28 cities/$299
- additional flights $100

Japan   **Japan Airlines**
                                  Welcome to Japan
                                  www.japanair.com
                                  800-525-3663
- $200 for 2 coupons/additional coupons are $100
- minimum of 2/maximum of 5 coupons
- good for flights within Japan
- valid 60 days

Latin America   **Avensa**
                                  Air Touring Pass
                                  www.avensa.com.ve
                                  800-428-3672
- coupons are $50-$200 ea.
- coupons must be purchased outside Latin America
- flights to Mexico, Central and South America

                                  Aviateca and Taca
                                  Visit Central America
                                  www.grupotaca.com
- flights to Mexico and Central America
- price is variable
- minimum of 2/maximum of 8 coupons
- valid 60 days

Malaysia   **Malaysia Airlines**
                                  Visit Malaysia Pass
                                  www.malaysiaairlines.com

800-421-8641

- 5 coupon pass $99
- travel within the Malaysian Peninsula
- valid 21 days

Mexico   **Aeromexico**
                                    Mexiplan
                                    www.aeromexico.com
                                    800-237-6639

- minimum of 3/no maximum of coupons
- flights $70-$170 depending on distance
- valid 1 year
- flights within Mexico

                                    Mexicana Airlines
                                    Discover Mexico
                                    www.aaeros.com/mexicana.html
                                    800-531-7921

- minimum 3 coupons
- 2 coupons can be used on international segments
- separate passes for beaches, interior and Caribbean
- additional cities can be added
- valid 2 days minimum - 45 day maximum

Morocco   **Royal Air Moroc**
                                    Discover Morocco
                                    800-344-6726

- 4 coupons $149/6 coupons $169
- valid 6 months

Netherlands   **Northwest/KLM**
                                    Passport to Europe
                                    www.nwa.com
                                    800-374-7747

- all KLM flights go through Amsterdam
- 3 flights within Europe $330-$405
- international flight must be Northwest or KLM

New Guinea

Air Niugini
Adventure Pass
www.airniugini.com.pg
714-752-5440

- 4 coupon pass/$299/additional coupons $75

New Zealand

Air New Zealand
Explorer Pass
www.airnz.com
800-262-1234

- 3 flights $240/additional flights $75 ea.
- minimum 3 flights/ maximum 8 flights
- valid 1 year
- Ansett's Visit Australia Pass and Quantas' Australian Passes include New Zealand
- see Australia for additional possibilities

North America

Most North American Airlines offer Air Passes that are only available to non-U.S. or non-Canadian passport holders. These passes must be purchased outside the U.S. in the departure country. Current information on these passes is best obtained from a travel agent in that country.

Continental/Air Canada
Continental/Air Canada Airpass
www.continental.com
800-776-3000

- 3 coupons with up to 8 extensions
- valid up to 60 days

- travel within USA and Canada
- Mexico, Hawaii, and Alaska at extra charge

Canadian Airlines
Canadian Airlines Airpass
www.cdnair.ca
800-426-7000

- Canada, USA, Yukon and Hawaii
- valid for 60 days
- up to 8 extensions possible

American Airlines
wwwr1.aa.com
Visit USA Fares
800-433-7300

- minimum purchase of 2 segments
- up to 8 additional segments possible

America West Airlines
America West Tristate Airpass
www.americawest.com
800-235-9292

- travel within Arizona, California and Nevada
- valid up to 60 days
- up to 12 extensions at $50 each

Delta Air Lines
www.delta-air.com
800-241-4141

- 3 coupons valid for 60 days within the USA
- up to 10 extensions possible
- Alaska, Bermuda, Hawaii, Mexico, and the Caribbean

Northwest Airlines
www.nwa.com
800-225-2525

- 3 flight coupons valid for 60 days within USA

- up to 8 extensions possible
- Jamaica, Hawaii, Puerto Rico, Mexico, and Dominican Republic are available at an extra charge

Southwest Airlines
Freedom USA Pass
www.southwest.com
210-617-1221

- pass can only be purchased in Australia, New Zealand, Germany, Israel, and the UK

United Airlines
Visit USA Airpass
www.ual.com
(800) 241-6522

- 3 flight coupons valid for 60 days
- up to 8 extensions possible
- travel on the routes of United and United Express
- travel to Canada, Mexico, San Juan, and Alaska
- travel to Hawaii at an extra charge

Norway

Broathens Safe
Visit Norway Pass
Nettvik.no/terminalen/braathens
800-722-4126

- coupons $70 within North Norway or South Norway
- coupons $140 between North and South Norway
- requires round-trip from North America on SAS

Paraguay

Air Paraguay
Visit South America
800-677-7771

- U.S. to Paraguay plus 2 cities $1,100
- valid 30 days

Peru

Faucett
Visit Peru Pass
800-334-3356

- unlimited travel $250
- valid 90 days
- no backtracking

Aeroperu
Visit South America
www.aero-peru.com
800-777-7717

- $60 to $70 per coupon
- extra flights $100
- travel within Peru
- valid 30 days

Aeroperu
SudAmerica Pass
www.aero-peru.com
800-777-7717

- Fly Aeroperu from Miami to Lima
- $1,299 for 6 coupons
- extra flights $100
- minimum of 6/no maximum
- valid 60 days

Philippines

Philippine Airlines
Visit the Philippines
www.philippineair.com
800-435-9725

- 4 coupons are $155/10 coupons are $198
- valid length of international ticket
- minimum of 4 coupons/maximum of 10

Scandinavia	**SAS**
	Visit Scandinavia Pass
	www.flysas.com
	800-221-2350

- coupons $80-$420
- maximum 6 coupons
- flights between Norway, Sweden, Denmark and Finland
- requires a round-trip ticket from North America on SAS or British Midlands Airlines
- valid 90 days

Nordic Air Pass
Finnair
www.us.finnair.com
800-950-5000

- coupons are$90-$170 ea.
- minimum of 4/ maximum of 10 coupons
- can be purchased in U.S. or Scandinavia
- travel to Scandinavia and Denmark

South Africa	**South African Airways**
	Africa Explorer
	800-722-9675

- 4 coupons $149/6 coupons $169
- valid 6 months

South America	**Areoperu**
	Sudamerica Pass
	800-777-7717

- 10 flights $1,299 (depends upon season)
- flights to 10 South American cities
- flights depart from Miami

Aeroperu
Visit South America

www.aero-peru.com
800-777-7717
- for details see Peru

Varig, Aerolineas Argentinas
MercoSur Airpass
www.aerolineas.com
800-333-0276
- fly in on a sponsoring airline
- $225-$875 depending on distance flown
- flights to Argentina, Brazil, Chile, Paraguay, and Uruguay
- valid 30 days

Lan Chile Airlines
South American Airpass
www.lanchile.com
800-735-5526
- minimum of 4 flights/maximum of 8
- sold in conjunction with international ticket
- priced by zones/$80 to $350
- flights to Santiago, Caracas, Bogota, Guayaquil, Rio, Sao Paulo, Lima, La Paz, Santa Cruz, Montevideo, Buenos Aires, and Easter Island

Southeast Asia

Thai Airways
ASEAN Circle Trip Fares
www.thaiairwayss.com
800-426-5204
- Indonesia, Malaysia, Philippines, Singapore, Thailand, and Vietnam
- two—six stopover plans
- three days to three months at each location

South Pacific

Air Promotion Systems
Visit The South Pacific Pass

www.pacificislands.com
310-670-7302

- $175-$320 per segment
- flights cover the South Pacific
- variety of airlines involved
- minimum of 2/no maximum

Air Niugini
Visit South Pacific Air Pass
www.airniugini.com.pg
949-752-5440

- minimum of 2/no maximum for coupons
- $220 per segment
- valid 90 days
- flights to New Guinea and Australia

Quantas
South Pacific Pass
www.qantas..com
800-227-4500

- basic pass $160 ea.
- minimum of 4 flights/maximum of 8
- travel between Australia/New Zealand/Fiji

Air Pacific
Pacific Air Pass
800-677-4277

- price range $150-$300
- valid 60 days

Polynesian Airlines
Polypass
www.polynesianairlines.co.nz
800-677-4277

- 345days unlimited travel/$999
- Samoa/Pago Pago/Fiji/Cook Islands

- add Tahiti/$100
- one stop each in Australia and New Zealand

Air Fiji
Discover Fiji Pass
www.airfiji.net
800-677-4277

- 4 flights for $236/additional flights $$70
- flights are within Fiji
- valid 30 days

Solomon Airlines
Discover Solomon Pass
www.pacificislands.com/airlines
800-677-4277

- 4 flights within 30 days/$236
- additional flights/$50

<u>Spain</u>

Iberia Airlines
Visit Spain Pass
www.iberia.com
800-772-4642

- 4 coupon pass $249-$299 (seasonal)
- additional flights $50
- valid 60 days

Spanair
Spain Pass
www.spanair.com
888-545-5757

- coupons start at $180 for 3
- one coupon minimum/ no maximum
- use for travel within Spain
- valid 90 days

Switzerland

Swissair
www.swissair.com
800-221-4750
- details given under Austria

Thailand

Thai Airways
Amazing Thailand Pass
www.thaiairways.com
800-426-5204
- 4 flights $179/additional flights $50
- maximum of 8 flights/maximum of 24
- valid for 90 days

Venezuela

Avensa Airlines
Avensa Airpass
www.avensa.com.ve
800-428-3672
- 45 days of unlimited travel/$70 per segment
- 27 destination cities
- minimum 4 segments

■ UNITED STATES REGIONAL PASSES

Some U.S. airlines offer special passes to u.s. citizens willing to purchase multiple tickets in advance. Although these tickets usually provide a substantial discount, they are normally non-refundable. Any tickets not used within the time restrictions become worthless. These programs are in a constant state of flux, so be sure to call and check before making any plans. Kiwi Airlines suspended service in 1999, but is still listed because they insist they will return.

America West
America West Value Pack
www.americawest.com
800-235-9292

- 4 one-way coupons/$299
- limited West Coast travel area — valid 1 year

Delta Airlines
Comair Weekend Traveler
www.delta-air.com
800-532-4777

- 4 coupons/$299
- over 500 miles requires 2 coupons

Kiwi Airlines (service suspended)
800-538-5494

- Atlanta/Tampa/$771 -10 one-way coupons
- Orlando/West Palm Beach/$771 -10 one-way coupons
- Newark/Atlanta/$1,101 -10 one-way coupons
- Newark/Chicago/$1,101 -10 one-way coupons
- Newark/ Orlando/$1,281 -10 one-way coupons
- Newark/ Tampa/$1,281 -10 one-way coupons
- Newark/ West Palm Beach/$1,281 -10 one-way coupons
- Chicago/ Orlando/$1,281 -10 one-way coupons
- Chicago/ Tampa/$1,281 -10 one-way coupons
- Chicago/ West Palm Beach/$1,281 -10 one-way coupons

Internet Resources

Resources on the Internet are boundless. An entire book could be written about the various sources available on the Internet. I realize that a detailed examination of the Internet is beyond the scope of this particular volume. However, since the Internet is such a valuable tool, I hope to give you enough knowledge so that you can begin to explore its possibilities.

■ INTERNET 101

In its simplest form "the Internet" refers to the connection of the world's computers, usually by telephone lines, into a giant network. Anyone with a home computer, a modem, and a telephone line can begin to tap into this network of computers. In order to be connected to this network of computers, you must pay a charge to an Internet provider. The most common providers are your local telephone company, AT&T, America Online, and CompuServe. These providers charge a nominal fee, usually 20 - $40 a month to provide this service.

Once a provider to the Internet connects you, you need an inexpensive computer software program called a browser to help you roam or "surf" from place to place. The two most popular browser programs are Netscape Navigator and Microsoft Internet Explorer. These browser programs are loaded on your personal computer. When you are ready to go online, you open your browser program and it connects you to the Internet through your modem, across the telephone line to your Internet provider, and onto the Internet. Your Home Page comes up and asks you for an address or URL.

When your computer asks you for a URL, it is saying, "Where do you want to go?" or "Please give me an address or location to investigate." Every location on the Internet has an address or Uniform Resource Locator (URL) so that it can be accessed. The URL is made up of a long confusing combination of letters and punctuation marks to identify a particular address. The 1st series of numbers and punctuation are known as the Protocol. Without getting into technical jargon, the Protocol simply explains how you wish to have the information transferred to your computer. The Internet supports the following Protocol URL types:

- http://   opens a World Wide Web page
- ftp://   File Transfer Protocol
- telnet://   connects to a telnet server
- gopher://   connects to a gopher server
- news: connects to a Usenet group
- file://   opens a file
- mailto   sends an e-mail message

■ THE URL

The only URL we are concerned with for the purpose of investigating airfare bargains is http://, which allows us access to the World Wide Web (www). The World Wide Web is, by far, the most popular part of the Internet and it is where we will go to look for discount airfares. The World Wide Web is such a popular location that unless we tell our browser program differently, this is where it will automatically take us. As we begin to search the Internet and are asked for a URL, we don't even have to type in http://www. Our browser just assumes that's where we want to go until we tell it differently. If you are using Netscape Communicator or Netscape Navigator, it is not necessary to include www. or the .com portions of the URL.

■ SEARCHING

When your browser connects you to the Internet, the first page it opens is the browser home page. There may be several things happening on this page, but the elements you are seeking are the search or location box and the search button. By placing your cursor in the location or URL box, clicking, and typing a location, you tell the browser where you wish to go. By clicking on the search button, or icon, you tell it to go there now. Your browser then begins seeking the requested address, and you can follow its progress by watching the bottom of the open window. That is all that's necessary to search the World Wide Web.

At this point you may ask the question, "What do I need to type into the location box?" You can type a specific location such as http://www. AmericanAirlines.com/, or something as simple as "airlines." As you probably can imagine "airlines" will get you thousands of possible locations, or hits, while a more specific location will greatly narrow your search. The World Wide Web is so vast that you need some help narrowing your search, or most of your online time will be wasted going from location to location never finding the exact object of your search.

■ SEARCH ENGINES

Search engines are the telephone books of the Internet. They help you find the exact location or subject you are seeking. As I said initially, when your browser opens onto the Internet, it opens onto its home page. This is your browser's home page. It does not have to be yours. The World Wide Web has several special searching pages, called "search engines" and you can tell your browser to open initially on one of these pages rather than its own home page. You can do this by selecting a new home page from the menu of your browser's home page. Here is a list of some of the most popular search engines:

- AltaVista
- Excite
- Hotbot
- Infoseek
- Lycos
- Yahoo
- About
- Webcrawler

Each of these search engines, or phone books, has a different database and different ways to search for information. Try them all before settling on your own particular preference. There are also some special search engines that, instead of searching the Internet for a requested URL, search other search engines. These are usually known as "meta-search tools." Some of the most popular are:

- MetaCrawler
- All-In-One
- E-Z Find
- Metasearch

If you are using a search engine to search the web for a topic, you are searching that particular engine's database. A program called "crawler" automatically collects a search engine's database. Each engine's crawler program has a different name (Scooter on AltaVista and Slurp on HotBot) and searches the entire www over a different period of time. When they find new or changed documents, they scan the information and add it to the services database.

On the other hand, if you are using a search engine's topic directory you are exploring information that has been selected and classified by people working for the service. As a result, you get fewer hits, but the hits you get are usually better quality.

The search engines you will be using to search the www do not allow you to do *field searches* in the traditional sense. With a conventional database you can search an author's name and get a list of his books, then search his name and get biographical information on the author himself, or use a Periodical database and locate articles written about the author. Field searches, if they are even available on the www, will return a jumble of hits lacking any overall organization. Often the number of hits is simply overwhelming.

In order to be effective at searching the www, you must become adept at selecting a correct, unique keyword. Learning to select the proper keywords will take some trial-and-error practice, but will improve your success rate astronomically. Here are some hints for selecting successful keywords.

- Use a specific, unique keyword. A search of the word cardinal, for example, will turn up hundreds of hits on birds, Catholic Church officials, and baseball players from St. Louis. The search will have to be much more specific.
- Check your spelling. Many failures are simply a result of spelling errors.
- Use set-searching techniques. Set-searching refers to the ability of some search engines to re-search the hits of your initial search. This is usually accomplished by adding another keyword and selecting "search only these results."

- Use a thesaurus approach. You may have to restart your search several times. After your initial query, you may notice some words that are common to the sites you are seeking. Restart your search using these words. This is similar to using a thesaurus. If the synonym we are seeking doesn't show on the first search, we use some of those words to search again.
- Check your case. Search engines vary on how they deal with case-sensitive names. Will a search of POP get you sites dealing with computer Post Office Protocol or hits that are more concerned about fatherhood.

While Natural Language searching is often the best approach for web neophytes, frequently you will require a more precise searching technique.

■ THE BOOLEAN BOOGIE

Have you ever had a friend tell you that they wasted an entire evening "surfing the web" and never, ever came upon anything of value? The www is unbelievably huge and the key to finding what you are looking for is simple; you must understand and use search strategies to narrow your search. It is much better to take the time in the beginning to learn how your search engine uses "Boolean operations" than to spend endless hours pouring over unwanted page hits. You use the Boolean operators AND, OR, NOT, and NEAR to narrow or fine-tune your web search.

For more sophisticated technical searching you need to become adept at handling Boolean modifiers. There are four commonly used Boolean modifiers: AND, OR, NOT, and NEAR. Different search engines handle their use in various ways, but here are some general rules:

⇒ **AND**—This modifier allows use of more than one keyword, and they must all appear for a hit to be chosen. This is the most effective way to limit your search and reduce hits. The following search illustrates locating facts about 14th century European painting.

- painting AND European AND 14th century
- + painting + European + 14th century

- painting European 14th century and select "all the words" from the drop down menu.

⇒ **OR**—This modifier allows you to widen a search returning too few hits. Keep in mind this is the default setting for most search engines. The following search illustrates locating facts about George Washington the 1st U.S. President.

- George Washington OR 1st U.S. President
- George Washington 1st U.S. President
- George Washington 1st U.S. President and select "any of the words" from the drop down menu.

⇒ **NOT**—This modifier allows you to exclude some results from the search. If you are investigating snakes, you are probably not interested in an English comedy troupe. The following search illustrates locating facts about pythons.

- python NOT monty
- python -monty
- python AND NOTmonty

⇒ **NEAR** —This modifier allows you to search for multiple keywords that might appear in the same document. Currently only AltaVista and Lycos have NEAR search capability. The following search illustrates locating facts about NBA star Michael Jordan's short baseball career.

- Michael Jordan NEAR Baseball

Hint: Always type the Boolean modifiers in all caps. The negative sign is always directly preceding the second word with no space between them.

■ POPULAR SEARCH ENGINES

- **AltaVista**   **www.altavista.com**
  powerful with large database updated daily
  allows simple and advanced searches, most popular
- **Excite**   **www.excite.com**
  sophisticated, concept-based searching
  no need to enter specific keywords-uses plain English
  large topic directory, updated weekly

excellent topic directory called channels
searchable travel database

- **Lycos**   **www.lycos.com**
  Easy to use, excellent multimedia database
  best for travel guides and road maps
- **HotBot**   **www.hotbot.com**
  easy to use drop-down Boolean menu
  fastest searches easy to modify a search
  allows special search terms called Meta-words for
  advanced searches
- **Infoseek**   **www.infoseek.com**
  large, easy-to-use database
  allows for set searching
  easy access to Deja News
  does not allow use of Boolean modifiers
  advanced searches by using Ultraseek
- **Yahoo!**   **www.yahoo.com**
  Web's most detailed topic directory with subtopics and
  sub-subtopics
  small, but well categorized, database
  excellent list of search engines available
  uses humans to create database
- **About**   **www.about.com**
  like Yahoo, uses humans to create database
  the choice for searching travel information on the Web
  best source for Internet special fares from airlines

Hint: Use the appropriate menu in your browser to have your favorite search engine automatically become your browser's home page.

- **Netscape**: Select Options, then Preferences, then Appearance, and enter the complete (including http://) address of your favorite search engine.
- **Microsoft Explorer:** Select View, then Options, then Navigations, then Start Page, then select Use Current.

Make sure you are at your favorite location before making the selection.

Hint: Be sure to master the simple operations of saving or *bookmarking* your favorite sites so you easily return to them. With the Netscape browser this is as simple as selecting add Bookmark from the Bookmark menu.

For the pros and cons of all these search engines, a good place to start is a document understanding www search Tools at URL http://www.indiana.edu/~librcsd/search/

■ SUBJECT DIRECTORIES

Subject directories differ from search engines in that they contain a list of sites already compiled and organized by an individual or organization. Some of the larger search engines have subject directories as part of their home page. Some of the more popular subject directories are:

- Internet Public Library
- Lycos Sites by Subject
- Argus Clearinghouse
- Magellan
- CyberDewey

■ USENET

As an adjunct to www searching do not overlook the use of *Usenet Newsgroups.* Usenet is an immense series of bulletin boards called *newsgroups,* where anyone who wishes can post messages on any specific topics. These newsgroups are Internet conversations on every imaginable subject, and are very often an excellent source of information on airfare and travel bargains. These newsgroups are very similar to chat rooms with the exception that they are not live. In *newsgroups,* you read messages— they are called *articles*—and post replies if you are interested in the topic. Periodically, you can check to see whether anyone has replied to your comments.

There are two methods for searching *newsgroups.* With the exception of Lycos, most search engines will allow you to search newsgroups. One of my personal favorites is *Deja News* at www.dejanews.com. This site has very powerful searching capabilities, so be sure to give it a try. The second method for searching *newsgroups* is to use a newsreader program. There are many different newsreader programs available, and most are freeware. My personal favorite is YA NewsWatcher for Macintosh. This program will allow you to easily locate travel messages, give you the ability to post your travel inquiries anonymously, and avoid unsolicited e-mail called *spam*.

■ AMERICA ONLINE

If America Online is your Internet provider, always look over their travel section located on their main menu. Don't overlook the travel chat rooms and bulletin boards. Other travelers are often the best source for discount tips.

In 1997, America Online removed the easySABRE reservation system and now uses Preview Travel. Use Preview Travel as a starting point to obtain a basic idea of the current fare. You should be able to find a much better discount by using some of the Web sites I have given you.

■ COMPUSERVE

CompuServe is another large online service with a doorway to the Internet. As with America Online, always check the special travel forum and chat rooms. CompuServe also has a special airline reservation system called Worldspan Travelshopper. To use Travelshopper try the following from the main menu:

- Travel
- Schedule and reservations
- Worldspan Travelshopper
- Access Travel shopper
- Select passenger information
- Type in your name and pick passenger type along with special requests
- Press OK
- Select Flights & Fares
- Fill out needed information
- Select flights
- Select airport
- Select arrival airport

- Select the flight you want
- Select add flight
- Fill out according to your return flight
- Select flights
- Select the flight you want
- Select price
- Press OK- you should get a list of prices

■ INTERNET AUCTION SERVICES

Priceline.com: One of the most exciting and newest travel Web sites is called Priceline. Its simple, yet revolutionary idea is to let the consumers name the price they are willing to pay for airline tickets to a particular destination. The prospective ticket buyers post their request on the Internet with Priceline and guarantee their offer with a major credit card.

This service will provide an appealing new method for purchasing discounted airline tickets. You simply name the price you are willing to pay, and Priceline seeks a major airline willing to release unsold seats at that price. Within one day, and often within one hour, you learn whether an airline has agreed to your offer. If so, you are immediately notified of the airline and scheduling.

Although flights must originate in the U.S., the service is available for both international and domestic travel. This service will provide an exciting alternative for the flexible traveler who does not need to fly a specific airline on a specific day. Since Priceline is seeking unbooked seats, the service is perfect for the consumer who was unable to purchase tickets in advance or meet apex requirements. In addition, since the tickets came from unsold space, there are no blackout date restrictions.

With Priceline, you only get one free price request for any proposed trip. Any additional requests will cost $25 each. This means that before you post a request, you will have to do some research. As a reader of this book, you should have several ways to approach this research. Here is a possible plan of action:

- Call the airline or your travel agent and check the lowest available apex economy class fare.
- Check prices with your favorite consolidator

- Use an Internet service to locate the lowest available fare. One of my favorites, because of its ease of use, is lowestfare.com.

After you have completed your research, you should have a good idea what price would represent a true bargain airfare to your destination. At this point, simply log on to **priceline.com** and make your ticket request. Be sure to follow the prompts and enter your exact itinerary. The more flexible your itinerary, the better your chance of getting tickets at your price.

Before Priceline will process your ticket request, it must be guaranteed with a major credit card. You can furnish your credit card information over the Internet, or if you prefer, you can use a toll free telephone number (1-800-PRICELINE). Within one hour (24 hours for international flights) Priceline will notify you by e-mail if your offer has been accepted. This notification will advise you of the airline and routing.

Priceline uses major full-service U.S. airlines and their affiliates for their bookings. Flights may include one stop or connection and do not normally earn frequent-flyer miles.

Before you contact Priceline.com here are some things to consider:

- Priceline often doesn't find a flight at your requested fare and you must make additional requests at $25 each.
- Priceline is often inflexible about departure times and possible layovers.
- Priceline usually will not allow ticket refunds, ticket changes, or collection of frequent flyer miles.
- Priceline will usually add tax to your bid price.
- Priceline often recommends that your price bid be above the airlines lowest published apex fare. If this is the case why call Priceline? Simply take the airlines fare.

SkyAuction.com: In early 1999, another company entered the airfare auction business. SkyAuction.com offers all classes of flights to most popular destinations.

In order to use SkyAuction you become a registered user after completing a free form. After submitting the form, SkyAuction will e-mail you a customer ID number that you use to place your airfare bids. Most airfare bids will be kept on auction for one week.

SkyAuction also offers a "AutoBid" feature that allows you to place a maximum acceptable bid for an airfare. If someone outbids your initial bid, your bid will be incrementally increased until it is either accepted or you are outbid. One nice feature of the "AutoBid" method is all ties go to the person using it. You can also use an "AuctionWatch" feature to keep track of all your bids.

While the SkyAuction concept is unique, one limiting factor is the need to match up with their offered itineraries. However, they do fly to many popular tourist destinations, so it may be worth a try.

TravelBids.com: Here is a new wrinkle in the airfare auction business. With TravelBids, you set the price you are willing to pay for a ticket to a particular destination. Your bid is entered on the TravelBids Web site and travel agents then bid for your business. All bids are visible and can be checked at any time. You also have the ability to set the bidding period.

To initiate the procedure with TravelBids, you must first call an airline directly using an 800 number they supply. It is also possible to use the Internet to assist you in locating a bargain airfare. You locate the lowest fare you can find and make a reservation without paying. Then you pay the $5 listing fee with TravelBids and list your trip. At this point travel agencies who are pre-qualified with TravelBids begin to bid on your reservation.

At the end of the bidding period, the winning agent charges your credit card for the discounted airfare and sends you the tickets. Once you have already located a true bargain airfare, TravelBids claims they can then save you an additional 5 to 10%.

TravelBids offers some advantages over Priceline because they allow you to accumulate frequent flyer miles and ticket changes can be made if necessary. In addition, you know the exact price of your trip, including all fees and taxes.

YourPriceTravel.com: This service appears to be very similar to TravelBids. You locate the best price possible and then make the reservation without paying for the ticket. You then list the trip along with your discount bid at Your Price Travel. They then utilize wholesalers and consolidators to match, beat, or reject your bid. If your bid is accepted, they will charge your credit card for the discounted fare and send you your tickets.

■ SEARCHING BARGAIN AIRFARES

OK, is everyone still with me? I hope the Internet searching material was of value to some of you who are new to web searches. It should be pretty clear by now that a www search for bargain airfares is as simple as typing "discount airfares" into your search engine, and see where the search takes you. Often, a site will have links to other sites and your search goes on until you reach a dead end. Always bookmark valuable sites. It is always easier to throw away a bookmark, than to research a lost location.

Now, start looking for bargains and try to reduce this fare by checking with consolidators, travel agents, or charter operators. It is possible that somewhere on the "net," you got a tip or found a special price that was just what you wanted. More likely, you obtained the information that will assist you to get the real bargain by using one or more of the other strategies in this book. Remember, knowledge and flexibility are the keys to obtaining the true bargain airfares.

Here is one of the first Web sites you should check on the WWW if you are planning a trip. About.com has organized the dozens of Internet specials offered each week. These specials are grouped by departure cities. This site simply asks you which cities you might wish to depart from, and then lists all of the week's specials.

Since the airlines usually list their specials on Wednesday evenings, the best time to check the site would be Wednesday or Thursday night. Keep in mind that you are usually required to purchase before midnight Friday.

I realize that this is a complicated URL, so once you have located the site place a bookmark. Enter each character exactly as you see them in the URL. In August and September of 1999, this site was not in operation due to some internal problem. I have received a message from About.com stating that as soon as these problems have been corrected, the site will again be in operation. Here is the URL *I consider the single most valuable travel Web site on the Internet.* **http://www.airtravel.about.com/library/city/blcities.htm?PM=7 8_706_T&cob=home.**

Here are some of my other favorites that you can use as a starting point:

Global Discount Travel Services
http://lowestfare.com
This online reservation service promises a 20 % discount off the lowest published airfares on a major U.S. carrier. Its ease of use and ability to compare different itineraries make it the first site I check to get an idea about a particular bargain fare. This site is one of my personal favorites.

Internet Airfares
www.air-fare.com
This site is an excellent way to locate the lowest published airfare between 40 major U.S./Canadian destinations. Simply select your home city and the site will provide a listing of the lowest published fares to the other 39 cities. In addition you receive the flight restrictions. This site also lists fare cuts and special bargains. There is also a link to ticketing and reservations. This is a great site to locate the lowest published fare before using the book's strategies to obtain more substantial bargains.

Flifo Global
http://1travel.flifo.com
This site has a convenient search feature called FAREBEATER that allows you to search for Consolidated/Discounted airfares. It allows for both domestic and international fare searches. Once you have located this site be sure to check out this link to **http://www.onetravel.com/rules/rules.cfm**. This is one of my favorite locations on the Internet. It is part of 1travel.flifo.com and is called *Rules of the Air*. This terrific location provides specific information on airline "carriage rules." Here are some of the topics covered:

- Airport: check-in time limits
- Baggage: check-in time limits
- Baggage: identification and inspection
- Baggage: lost/damaged/delayed
- Fare decrease after ticket purchase

- Fare increase after ticket purchase
- Flight delays/cancellations/misconnections
- Oversold flights/denied boarding
- Passenger identification and inspection
- Refusal to transport
- Reservations: cancelled/double bookings/guaranteed
- Tickets: back-to-back/hidden city/throwaway

This site allows you to check any of 17 major carriers for their specific rules on any of these topics.

The Trip
http://thetrip.com

Here is a great site to use to investigate domestic airfares. Their "Trip Planner" feature will notify you of lower fares using alternate flights. This site also has an excellent "FlightTracker" to check on current flight status.

Smarter Living
http://www.smarterliving.com

This site is a good source for checking on any last minute Internet specials. Smarter Living summarizes Internet discount fares for twenty major airlines. They also provide a free newsletter and a "deal alert" section for the latest travel offers.

Budgetfares
http://www.resor24.com

Here is another site that can seek out low domestic and international airfares.

CheckAirFare
http://www.checkairfare.com

Here is a site devoted to last minute domestic flights with no advance and no minimum stay requirements. It is also a resource for business travelers interested in First or Business Class U.S. domestic and international fares.

Banana Travel

http://www.tvllink.com

Another site with a special search feature called "Cheap Fare Finder." This site can be useful to get an idea on the airfare although the fares I checked were a little on the high side.

Microsoft Expedia

http://expedia.msn.com

This is the "sign in" page for Microsoft's complete Online travel services.

Budget Travel Online

http://frommers.com

This is travel expert Arthur Frommer's Web site featuring articles and hints for saving on every type of travel. This is a good site if you are interested in a complete travel package.

Fodor's Travel Online

http://www.fodors.com

Fodor's complete travel service which provides an online forum for travelers to talk "shop."

Fare Mail

http://www.itn.net

ITN's Fare Mail is a site that we send you an e-mail when the price to any pre-selected destination reaches a price you have specified.

Tiss Services

http://www.travelsecrets.com

Online prices and reservations are available for both domestic and international flights; however, it is best used for international destinations. They advertise consolidator and bulk-negotiated airfares. They use a program called "faretracker" to notify you when an airline is offering a fare that matches your budget for any specified destination. This site provides some easy ways to check on youth/student/senior fares.

TravelHUB
http://www.travelhub.com
This Discount Airfare Network site claims to have the largest online database of consolidator fares.

Farebase
http://www.farebase.com
Here is a simple easy to use database that searches airline and travel agents for the lowest fare.

High Adventure Travel, Inc.
http://www.highadv.com
This site provides information on around-the-world and circle-pacific airfares. It is also a great source for all types of discount airfare information. The site includes an interesting "Fare Builder" feature that allows you to construct your own specific routing. This feature is a great resource for building your own "around-the-world" itinerary, as well as the best site on the Internet to find bargain "one-way" fares.

■ CONSOLIDATOR SEARCH DATABASES

Here are my favorite Internet Consolidator Search Databases. Always try to use at least six or more of them if you are researching a low fare.

www.tiss.com

www.a-travel.com

www.flifo.com

www.economytravel.com

www.counciltravel.com

www.interworldtravel.com

www.aesu.com

www.airfarestore.com

www.airfare.com

www.traveldiscounts.com

www.air-fare.com

www.air4less.com

www.cheaptickets.com

www.travelteam.com

■ SPECIAL INFORMATION SITES

http://www.bestdiscountairfares.com
http://airsafe.com/
http://travel.state.gov/travel_warnings.html
http://www.bts.gov/oai/oai.html
http://airtravel.miningco.com/library/weekly/
http://AIR-online.com/
http://www.intrepidtraveler.com/
http://www.aircourier.org/
http://www.courier.org/
http://abcnews.go.com/sections/travel/
http://www.cnn.com/CNN/Programs/TravelGuide/
http://bestfares.com/
http://www.milehighclub.com/

■ MAJOR CRS'S

Amadeus	www.amadeus.com
Apollo	www.apollo.com
easySABRE	www.easysabre.com
SystemOne	www.sys1.com
Worldspan	www.worldspan.com

■ PROPRIETARY RESERVATIONS SYSTEMS

Internet Travel Network	www.int.com
Microsoft Expedia	www.exspedia.msn.com
Travelocity	www.travelocity.com
Yahoo Air Travel	www.yahoo.flifo.com

■ AIRLINE WEB PAGES

Here are a few of the airlines mentioned in this book. If you don't see the airline you are looking for go to
http://www.flyaow.com/airlines.htm

AccessAir	http://www.accessair.com
Aer Lingus	http://www.aerlingus.ie

Aeroflot	http://www.aeroflot.org/Aeroflot.html
Aeromexico	http://www.wotw.com/aeromexico
Air Canada	http://www.aircanada.ca
Air France	http://www.airfrance.fr
Air Jamaica	http://www.airjamaica.com
Air South	http://www.airsouth.com
Air Europa	http://www.easyspain.com
AirTran	http://www.airtran.com
Air New Zealand	http://www.airnz.com
Alaska	http://www.alaska-air.com
Alitalia	http://www.alitalia.com
Aloha	http://www.alohaair.com
America West	http://www.americawest.com
American	http://www.americanair.com
American Trans Air	http://www.ata.com
Ana All Nippon	http://www.ana.co.jp/index-e.html
Atlantic	http://www.atlanticairlines.com
British Airways	http://www.british-airways.com
British Midland	http://www.iflybritishmidland.com
Canadian	http://www.cdnair.ca
Cape Air	http://www.flycapeair.com
Carnival	http://www.carnivalair.com
Cathay Pacific	http://www.cathay-usa.com
CityBird	http://www.citybird.com
Continental	http://www.flycontinental.com
Debonair	http://www.debonair.co.uk
Delta	http://www.delta-air.com
Delta Express	http://www.delta-air/express/index/html
Eastwind	http://www.eastwindairlines.com
EasyJet	http://www.easyjet.com
El Al	http://www.elal.co.il
Finnair	http://www.us.finnair.com
Frontier	http://www.flyfrontier.com
GO	http://www.go-fly.com
Gulfstream	http://www.gulfstreamair.com

KLM	http://www.klm.nl
LOT	http://www.lot.com
Lufthansa	http://www.lufthansa.com
Mesa	http://www.mesa-air.com
MetroJet	flymetrojet.com
Mexicana	http://www.mexicana.com
Midway	http://www.midwayair.com
Midwest Express	http://www.midwestexpress.com
Mountain Air	http://www.mountainairexpress.com
National	http://www.nationalairlines.com
Northwest	http://www.nwa.com
PGA	http://www.pga.pt
ProAir	http://www.proair.com
Qantas	http://www.qantas.com
Reno	http://www.renoair.com
Ryanair	http://www.ryanair.ie
SAS Scandinavian	http://www.sas.se
Sabena	http://www.sabena.com
Shuttle America	http://www.shuttleamerica.com
Singapore	http://www.singaporeair.com
Southwest	http://www.southwest.com
Spanair	http://www.spanair.com
Spirit	http://www.spiritair.com
Sun Country	http://www.suncountry.com
Swissair	http://www.swissair.com
Tower Air	http://www.towerair.com
TWA	http://www.twa.com
United	http://www.ual.com
US Airways	http://www.usairways.com
ValuJet	http://www.valujet.com
Vanguard	http://www.flyvanguard.com
Virgin Atlantic	http://www.fly.virgin.com
Virgin Express	http://www.virgin-express.com
VLM	http://www.vlm-air.com
Western Pacific	http://www.westpac.com

■ OTHER BOOKMARKS

Here are some other bookmarks taken from the travel folder on my computer. I hope you can make use of them.

http://www.airhitch.org/
http://www.airtech.com/
http://www.bestfares.com/
http://www.aircourier.org/
http://www.courier.org/
http://www.webflyer.com/
http://inetserver.guides.com/acg/
http://www.priceline.com/
http://SkyAuction.com/
http://www.travelbids.com/
http://www.checkairfare.com/
http://www.iatan.org/
http://abcnews.go.com/sections/travel/
http://www.cnn.com/CNN/Programs/TravelGuide/index.html
http://www.obs-us.com/obs/english/books/pg/pg495b.htm
http://www.atwtraveler.com/weblist.htm
http://www.highadv.com/
http://www.travelsmith.com/
http://www.tvllink.com/flycheap.htm
http://www.americanexpress.com/travel/
http://www.airtravel.com/airfare.html
http://www.americanexpress.com/travel/
http://www.news.travelgram.com/travelgram/
http://www.travel.org/airlines.html
http://www.intrepidtraveler.com
http://www.frommers.com/
http://www.tvllink.com/index.htm
http://savvytraveler.com/
http://www.travelminute.com/mall.htm
http://www.discountmexicotravel.com/
http://www.sta-travel.com/
http://www.demon.co.uk/

http://www.mta-tvl.com/
http://www.swainaustralia.com/
http://aloha.8m.com/index.html
http://www.rohcg.on.ca/
http://www.egypttours.com/
http://www.princeton.edu/
http://www.covesoft.com/
http://www.metro.net/
http://www.airdiscounter.com/
http://www.ultrainfoseek.com/

■ SIGN OFF

The Internet, and the www in particular, is a great place to begin your search for bargain airfares. Starting here, you can determine the listed price and the price range of a good discount fare. Use this information as a starting point.

For information about other aspects of air travel be sure to check my Web site at **http://www.bestdiscountairfares.com**. Here are some of the links and topics covered at that site:

- online maps
- worldwide weather conditions
- airline safety statistics
- where to file complaints against airlines
- online currency converters
- Passport and Visa information
- travel and health advisories
- campground and camping directories
- hostel and hotel information
- frequent flyer updates

Upstart Airlines

If you're old enough to remember People Express out of New York City to Europe, you will remember that at one time it was possible to fly across the Atlantic for $99. People Express was the original upstart "no frills" airline. After a few years, and continuing pressure from the large carriers, their operation folded. The general industry sentiment was that the upstarts couldn't compete with big guys.

In recent years, however, the industry maxim has been taking its lumps. A new group of upstarts has begun flying low-cost, no-frills flights across the U.S. These new discount upstarts are generally known as "low fare" or "niche" carriers. Many of these airlines offer rates up to 50% off standard fares for short (2 or 3 hour) flights with no meals, reserved seats, or frequent flyer miles. Their service is usually to out-of-the-way airports, and often you have to handle your own baggage if you need to transfer.

In the aftermath of the 1996 ValuJet crash in Florida that killed 110 people, and the subsequent shut down of the airline because of safety concerns, upstart or discount airlines have been attracting more than their normal share of attention in the press. ValuJet later applied to the Federal Aviation Administration and was allowed to resume flying, albeit on a limited schedule.

Although safety statistics do not seem to show a clear correlation between fares and safety, it does seem to be a clear public perception. Although the FAA is quick to assert that all U.S. Airlines meet the same strict safety codes and that they remain the world's safest, there are several no-frill upstarts with questionable safety records. To check a carrier's rate of accidents, you can contact the FAA's Flight Standards Service in Oklahoma City, OK (Phone 405-954-4391).

Safety records aside, over 20 upstart, discount airlines have begun operating in the U.S. in the past eight years. The upstarts now carry over 15% of domestic air passengers. Some of these discount airlines have top safety records and top-notch customer satisfaction ratings.

For the customer who can accept less service in return for rock-bottom prices, these new airlines fit the bill. In addition, some of the upstart carriers don't burden the passenger with all the ticket restrictions of a major airline. Often they are very flexible about ticket changes and length of stay. Customer satisfaction as to on-time flights and boarding time has generally been highly rated.

Some of these upstart airlines are not listed in the computer reservation systems of many travel agents, so you need to ask specifically for them if you go through a travel agent.

For those of you who wish to explore this option on your own, here is a list of some of the more prominent upstarts. This list is not all-inclusive and only lists some of the cities these airlines serve. If they might be of interest to you, call their toll-free number and check out their schedule.

■ MAJOR U.S. UPSTARTS

American Trans Air
1-800-225-2995

http://www.ata.com

Based in Indianapolis with flights to New York, Los Angeles, Miami, Chicago, Hawaii, San Juan, and Ireland. As North America's largest Charter airline, ATA operates a flexible and efficient fleet of 24 Boeing 727s, 9 Boeing 757s, and 16 Lockheed L-1011 aircraft.

America West Airlines
800-235-9292

www.americawest.com

America West operates from hubs in Phoenix, Las Vegas, and Columbus with a fleet of 116 aircraft. They have over 800 daily departures to 51 domestic destinations. America West's route system includes most major destinations across the United States, with additional destinations in Mexico and Canada. The airline's fleet consists of, Boeing 757s, Boeing 737s, Airbus A320s, and Airbus A319s.

AirTran Airlines
800-247-8726

www.airtran.com

Serving cities in the Northeastern and Southeastern U.S. from their hub in Atlanta, AirTran has over 280 daily departures. Their 48 aircraft consist of McDonnell Douglas DC-9s and Boeing 737 aircraft.

AccessAir
877-462-2237

www.accessair.com

Access Air serves six cities including New York, Colorado Springs., and Los Angeles. Their fleet consists of Boeing 737-200 advanced twin-engine jets.

Frontier
800-432-1359

www.flyfrontier.com

Frontier currently operates a fleet of ten 136-passenger Boeing 737-300 jets and nine smaller 737-200s, to New York, Atlanta, Orlando, Dallas/Ft. Worth, Phoenix, Los Angeles, San Francisco, Seattle, Portland, Las Vegas, and other domestic U.S. cities.

Kiwi International (service suspended 1999)
1-800-538-5494

Based in Newark, New Jersey with flights to Atlanta, Chicago, Orlando, and San Juan. Kiwi insists they will return to service.

National Airlines
888-757-5387

www.nationalairlines.com

Based in Las Vegas, National Airlines offers daily nonstop 757-200 jet flights between its Las Vegas hub and Los Angeles, Chicago, New York and San Francisco.

Southwest Airlines
Headquarters in Dallas, Texas
1-800-435-9792
http://www.southwest.com

With nearly 300 airplanes serving over 50 cities nationwide, Southwest is the leader and granddaddy of the upstart or low-fare airlines. They fly nearly 2,500 daily flights to 29 states.

Spirit
800-772-7117
www.spiritair.com

Spirit serves 14 cities including Atlantic City, New York, and Orlando. The Spirit Airlines all-jet fleet consists of McDonnell Douglas DC-9's and MD-80's.

Sun Country
800-752-1218
www.suncountry.com

Sun Country operates a fleet of twelve 727-200s, and four DC-10s. Service is from Minneapolis/St. Paul to San Diego, Miami, Boston, Dallas/Ft. Worth, Houston, Las Vegas, Los Angeles, New York-JFK, Orlando, Phoenix, San Antonio, San Francisco, Seattle, Washington D.C., and seasonal service to Cancun, the Caribbean, and Costa Rica.

Tower Air
1-800-348-6937
http://www.towerair.com

Tower Air provides 747 flights to and from J.F.K. International Airport. Tower Air serves New York, Los Angeles, San Francisco, Miami, Paris, San Juan, and Tel Aviv.

■ REGIONAL PLAYERS
Atlantic Airlines
800-879-0000

www.atlanticairlines.com

Gulfstream
800-525-0280
www.gulfstreamair.com

MetroJet
888-638-7653
www.flymetrojet.com

Midway
800-446-4392
www.midwayair.com

ProAir
800-939-9551
www.proair.com

Vanguard
800-826-4827
www.flyvanguard.com

■ EUROPEAN UPSTARTS
AB Airlines
800-458-8111
+44 1849 453312 UK
www.abairlines.com

With a fleet of Boeing 737-300s and BAC 1-11 500s, the British AB Airlines offers low-fare option for flights between Barcelona, London, Nice, and Shannon.

Air Europa
800-327-1225
+34 - 971 178 100
www.g-air-europa.es

Air Europa is a Spanish low-fare airline with flights between Madrid, London, Paris, and the Canary Islands.

British Midland

800-788-0555

01332 854274 UK

www.iflybritishmidland.com

British Midland currently operates flights to over 30 European destinations, carrying over 6 million passengers per year and is London Heathrow's second largest UK operator. British Midland destinations include: Amsterdam, Belfast, Brussels, Budapest, Copenhagen, Dublin, Edinburgh, Frankfurt, Hamburg, London, Munich, Nice, Paris, Prague, and Warsaw.

City Bird

888-248-9247

www.citybird.com

City Bird is a Belgian Airline providing affordable non-stop or direct service between the United States and Brussels. Their fleet of Boeing 767-300ERs, and McDonnell Douglas-MD11s offer flights with connections via Brussels to and from more than 50 European Cities.

Debonair

(+44) (0)541 500 300, UK

www.debonair.co.uk

Debonair operates a fleet of twelve British Aerospace 146 aircraft and two Boeing 737s. Debonair operates scheduled services between London Luzon Airport and Barcelona, Madrid, Munich, Nice (summer only), Paris, and Rome.

In addition to its independent route network, Debonair has been contracted by Lufthansa Cityline to operate services on their behalf from their Munich hub starting spring 1999. Debonair also flies for SwissAir from Zurich to Bologna and Venice.

Easyjet

+44-0870-6-000-000 UK

www.easyjet.com

EasyJet operates the Boeing 737-300, and has ordered 12 brand new aircraft. Some of these have been delivered, and the total 12 will have been delivered by the end of the year. Fifteen b737-700 are also on order (delivery by the year 2003) with a further fifteen on option.

They fly 27 European routes from three bases at London Luton, Liverpool, and Geneva. Some of their destinations include: Belfast, Edinburgh, Amsterdam, Zurich, Nice, Athens, Madrid, and Barcelona.

GO

0845 60 54321 UK

www.go-fly.com

GO's current fleet of 12 Boeing 737-300s are twin engine jets with 148 seats. Their current route schedule includes Barcelona, Bologna, Copenhagen, Edinburgh, Faro, London, Lisbon, Madrid, Malaga, Milan, Munich, Prague, Rome and Venice.

LTU International Airways

Reservations: (888) 888-0200

www.ltu.com

With a current fleet of 15 Boeing 757-200s, 6 Boeing 767-300ERs, and 6 Airbus A330 aircraft, LTU schedules destinations worldwide to, and from Germany. They also provide service from Miami, Florida, to San José, Costa Rica, with flights on Monday and Wednesday. Rates start at $298rt.

Martinair

800- 627-8462

www.martinair.com

Martinair offers passengers low-fare alternatives to Europe. Their flights originate or terminate in Holland. In 1998, Martinair added service to and from Costa Rica providing not only transatlantic service between San Jos´e and Amsterdam, but Martinair service between Miami and Costa Rica.

Martinair offers Miami to San Jos´e, Costa Rica, for as low as $298 roundtrip, and Youth Perx special fares from Miami & Orlando to Amsterdam for as low as $298 roundtrip. These special fares are available for youth ages 12 - 26.

PGA

(161) 489 50 40 UK

www.pga.pt

PGA is presently flying to a total of 22 destinations in 8 countries (7 in Europe and 1 in northern Africa – Morocco), operating a fleet of 12 aircraft (6 Fokker and 6 Embraer). Some current PGA destinations include: Tenerife, Casablanca, Palma, Madrid, Lisbon, Barcelona, Nice, Lyon, and Manchester.

Ryanair

0870-333-1239 UK

www.ryanair.ie

Ryanair operates an all jet fleet of 24 Boeing 737 aircraft with an order for 45 new aircraft in place. They fly routes between Ireland, the UK, and 15 European cities. Their destinations include: Glasgow, Dublin, London, Liverpool, Paris, Oslo, Stockholm, Brussels, Frankfurt, Genoa, Pisa, and Venice.

Spanair

888-545-5757

www.spanair.com

Spanair uses the McDonnell Douglas-MD82/83/87, and the Boeing 767/300 ER. The current fleet is composed of 24 aircraft —17 MD-83, 3 MD-82, 2 MD-87, and 2 Boeing 767-300 ER.

The MD 80 Series are 170-seater planes usually used on flights between European airports, the Canary Islands and North Africa. The Boeing 767/300 ER is a 266-seater Spanair uses in its long range flights, especially those over the Atlantic.

Their current route schedule includes: Copenhagen, Estocolmo, London, Frankfurt, Washington, Havana, Buenos Aires, Rio de Janeiro, Sao Paulo, and Malabo.

Virgin Express

(0171) 744 0004 UK

www.virgin-express.com

Virgin Express operates a modern fleet of Boeing 737 jets (the 300 and 400 series) with daily scheduled flights from Brussels to Milan, Rome, Madrid, Barcelona, Nice, Copenhagen, Shannon, all three major London airports, with coach service between Brussels and Rotterdam.

VLM

+44 (0) 171 476.6677 UK

www.vlm-air.com

Currently, VLM operates 6 Fokker50s. The Fokker50 is a 50 seat turboprop aircraft specifically built for short to medium haul routes. All VLM-Fokker50 have a 50-seat configuration, offering plenty of leg and head space for all passengers.

Their current routes include: Antwerp, Rotterdam, London, Manchester, Düsseldorf, and Luxembourg.

PART II

Specialized Tactics

Part II of this guide presents more sophisticated methods often used by the professional bargain airfare connoisseur. Although many of these methods may not be suited to your personality, temperament, or traveling attitude, you should be aware of them. Often, simply adding one of these tactics to your overall plan can increase your savings by an additional 10-50%. In fact, method #1 "bumps", has the *ability to save you* 100% *of your ticket cost.*

O.K., fasten your seat belts, put your tray in the upright position, and let's get into the real "nuts and bolts" of saving on an airline ticket.

Bumps

I've chosen to discuss "bumps," first, in Part II, because it is #1 in the hearts of the true discount seeker. No single method has the possibility for greater savings than the bump. Last year nearly one million airline passengers received discounted or free travel in return for volunteering to be bumped. This is the ultimate strategy for the real "pro," and here's how it works.

Nearly all airlines routinely overbook their domestic flights. I have already discussed the airlines' aversion to unsold seats. They know from experience that a certain number of passengers will not arrive to take any given flight. The obvious answer for the airline is to overbook, or oversell their available seats. The airlines have been at this for many years, and can pretty well gauge the number of "no-shows." As you might imagine, however, many times it is impossible for the airlines to hit this number right to the last passenger. Very often more passengers show up for a given flight than the seats they have available. This leads to a common problem for the airline.

Operating an airline is a very competitive business, and the last thing any airline wants is customer dissatisfaction, or "ill will." As a result, they have devised unique ways to handle this problem, and, in the end, have a satisfied customer. Their solution is called their "bump policy." For the discount minded traveler, it can work as the ultimate savings technique.

The Department of Transportation places certain requirements on the airlines, but even so, every airline's policy is a little unique. Most U.S. airlines follow Rule 240 which states that if you are involuntarily bumped from your ticketed flight and the airline is unable to get you to your destination on an alternative flight within one hour of your scheduled arrival time, the airline is obligated to pay you $400 cash or twice the one-way fare to your destination, whichever is less. All airlines are required to solicit volunteers for a later flight, before simply informing passengers that all seats are full on their particular flight.

To encourage volunteers, the airlines offer certain incentives. These incentives can involve free round-trip tickets for later use, discount coupons for later travel, cash, a free meal, and even an overnight hotel room if their next available flight doesn't leave until the following day. The most common incentive is for airline personnel to offer a bumped passenger a ticket on their next available flight to their destination and a free round trip ticket to any destination in the airline's route, for later use. The airlines hope that the added free ticket will more than compensate for the inconvenience of the delay in the passenger's travel plans.

As I mentioned earlier, each airline has its own policy. What you are offered as an incentive by a particular airline often will depend upon your ability to negotiate what you want. Sometimes an airline might offer you a first class ticket on their next available flight. Some airlines offer a voucher good for a discount on a future ticket. It really depends upon what you want, or in the case where you are involuntarily bumped, what you demand as compensation. The true discount airfare professional spends a little extra time hanging around the airport and knows each airline's "bump policy." He is also aware of certain flights that are consistently overbooked. This knowledge can be exchanged for tremendous savings in airline travel costs.

■ VOLUNTARY BUMPS

When too many passengers arrive for an oversold flight, the airline will ask for volunteers to give up their seats. If they have compiled a bump list, they will begin with those names. If there is no bump list, or if the overbooking extends beyond the bump list, the airline will announce that they are requesting volunteers. A volunteer will give up their seat on the flight in exchange for compensation and a seat on a later flight.

At this point, the airline will attempt to confirm you on their next scheduled flight with space available, regardless of the class of service. If this arrangement is not acceptable to you, they will attempt to confirm you on the flight of another airline—even if first class is the only space available.

In addition, the airline will offer you compensation in the form of a travel voucher, money, or both. The amount of the compensation is negotiated and determined by the airline. The exact compensation varies between airlines. For the most current information check the "Rules of the Air" section of my Web site at **bestdiscountairfares.com.**

For the original "Rules of the Air" Web site go to http://www.onetravel.com/rules/rules.cfm. Choose your airline, topic, and then select "Find Rule." This excellent site answers dozens of specific questions concerning Contract of Carriage rules for any given airline. These Carriage Rules are updated weekly, so check in occasionally to stay current.

Here are some additional considerations:

- Ask if the airline will provide you with a free meal, transportation, and a hotel room if you have an extended wait for the next available flight.
- If the airline offers you a free ticket for later use, always check the restrictions on that ticket. What is the time limit for its use? Can it be used during the airline's blackout periods? Will the compensation allow you to fly with no advance notice? Is it good for international, as well as, domestic travel? Can you reserve a seat on this later flight, or will you simply be placed on a standby list? Can the name on the ticket be transferred so another family member or friend can use the ticket?
- If you are the only volunteer and seem to have some bargaining clout, always ask in a congenial manner if you can be compensated with a first class ticket.

Here are the most recent statistics on voluntary bumps from the Department of Transportation:

AIRLINE	VOLUNTARY BUMPS
Delta	189,886
American	163,872
United	110,274
Northwest	98,147

US Airways	67,167
Southwest	60,802
Continental	54,513
America West	36,790
TWA	26,041
Alaska	19,532

■ INVOLUNTARY BUMPS

Occasionally an airline will simply inform a passenger that the flight is full and attempt to deny boarding. Be sure to remind the agent that Department of Transportation rules require them to board the plane and ask for bump volunteers before they deny you passage.

If you are denied boarding, the general rule for both domestic and international flights require the airline to compensate you for the value of that segment of your ticket—up to $200. This requirement is in effect if the airline can get you to your destination less than four hours later than your scheduled arrival. In the event that you arrive four or more hours later than your original arrival time, the compensation becomes two times the value of that segment of your ticket—up to $400.

These are the basic requirements for airlines departing from the United States. Departures from foreign countries have requirements that vary, and some offer no compensation whatsoever.

In case of an involuntary bump, be sure to ask all the appropriate questions about your compensation. Here are a few of the airlines with the best current policies.

America West offers a transferable free domestic round-trip.

Continental offers a free domestic round-trip that can be issued in anyone's name.

Delta offers a free domestic or Caribbean round-trip that is transferable to family members.

Northwest offers a transferable discount of up to $300 for domestic or international travel.

Southwest offers compensation vouchers equal to the value of your ticket, up to $200 for delays of two hours or less, and up to $400 for delays over four hours. This voucher can be issued in anyone's name and even reassigned, later, to another person.

TWA offers a free domestic round-trip that is non-transferable.

Here are the most recent statistics on involuntary bumps from the Department of Transportation.

AIRLINE	INVOLUNTARY BUMPS
Delta	9,639
Southwest	8,136
United	3,542
TWA	2,987
American	2,312
America West	1,536
Alaska	1,459
Northwest	1,117
US Airways	991
Continental	375

■ GENERAL RULES

Generally the airline will offer no compensation if they can get you to your destination within one hour of your scheduled arrival time. To be eligible for any compensation, the passenger must have a confirmed reservation for the flight and be in the boarding area before the check-in cutoff time. Keep in mind that international flights can have a check-in deadline up to two hours before flight time. The Department of Transportation does not require compensation to be given on flights with less than 60 passengers or on charter flights. To see the exact requirements for individual airlines, visit "Rules of the Air" at **bestdiscountairfares.com**.

Armed with this knowledge of the airlines' overbooking practices and bump policy, our next objective is to get bumped from a flight to a location we might want to visit later (at no cost, of course, using the free incentive tickets). How about Hawaii?

I know several people with more free tickets to Hawaii than they could ever use. How did they accumulate all these free flights? It's easy. They know of a particular flight, on a particular airline, at a particular time, that is regularly overbooked, and they knew what to do with that knowledge.

■ GETTING BUMPED

Once you have determined which flight, to your desired destination, has the greatest possibility for overbooking, buy a ticket for that flight. If you don't plan on actually making the trip, make sure the ticket you are holding is fully refundable.

Timely preflight check-in is critical to your success with this strategy. Keep in mind that the airlines have two check-in areas. The first check-in is at the ticket/baggage area and often has long lines unless you arrive several hours before departure time. The second check-in is located at the boarding lounge. This second check-in area is where any bumps or compensation will take place.

After confirming your flight and checking in (without luggage, of course, if you plan on being bumped), proceed immediately to the passenger check-in lounge. Be there when the ticketing personnel arrive to begin check-in for your flight. They will usually arrive about two hours prior to departure. Always be the first person in line. Bump compensation will go to the first to request it if the flight is only overbooked by a single seat. Explain that you are aware that your flight may be overbooked, and that you would like them to place your name on the list of volunteers to be bumped, if that becomes necessary. That's all there is to it. Your name will be placed on a list, and if it becomes necessary to bump certain passengers to a later flight, you will be called, notified, and compensated.

The final step is to negotiate the desired compensation. Knowledge of the airline's compensation policy is critical at this step. Be a prudent negotiator and know in advance what you are going to ask for in compensation. Carry a flight schedule so you can tell the agent what alternative flight you would like to be protected on by Rule 240. It's entirely possible to be bumped, receive free round-trip compensation for later use, take an alternative flight, and arrive at your destination before the originally scheduled flight.

Whenever possible try to get your free compensation round-trips to allow you to fly with no advance notice. This is not always possible, as you can imagine, but is valuable insurance for avoiding high, last minute fares if you later need to travel on short notice. While you're at it, why not ask for First Class? You won't always be awarded First Class tickets just because you ask for them, but if the airline is in a jam and needs bump volunteers it's often possible. You'll never know unless you ask for them.

If you are bumped from a flight and have to wait for an extended period of time for a substitute or alternative flight, always ask for a meal ticket to use while waiting. Often the airline will toss in some free drink, or headphone coupons, for use during your later flight.

After you have been bumped to a later flight, use the same strategies. Check in early, and hope to be bumped again. Double and triple bumps are not that uncommon on long, transcontinental trips with several connecting flights.

The more people in your party, the greater your chance to be selected for bumping if a flight is extremely overbooked. Although there may be four people in your group and each member will receive compensation, the airline will view your party as a single unit. They vacate four seats by bumping a single group. It simplifies their job and makes it quicker. They negotiate once instead of four times. The down side to this option is when only one seat is overbooked. In that case, you've missed an opportunity.

In addition to knowing which flights have a tendency to bump passengers, there are some additional steps you can take to increase the odds.

- Have you ever noticed the special news stories from the airport the day before Thanksgiving or the day before Christmas Eve? Book one of these flights.
- Why not schedule your trip late on a Friday afternoon when all the business travelers are trying to get home?
- How about your return ticket being on a Sunday night when all the working, nine to five, travelers are returning?
- Many business travelers like to leave on Monday mornings, so this is a real possibility.

- Flights between the hub areas of any airline have a tendency to be at, or near, capacity seating.
- Always watch the weather. Often severe weather or fog can cause cancellations which result in later flights being overbooked leading to bump opportunities.
- Know which airlines have the most liberal compensation for bumped passengers. Currently, TWA, Delta, Continental, and America West will usually award free round-trip tickets. Many of the other airlines compensate with discount coupons.
- Always call your travel agent the day before your departure and ask about seat availability. Tell your agent you have a friend who is also considering this trip, and ask if seats are still available. If your agent tells you all seats have been assigned, it's a good bet that the flight has been overbooked.

Some friends of mine use this bump strategy three or four times each year. They buy last minute refundable tickets to Hawaii on a Friday night "cattle car" flight that is habitually overbooked. They sign up to be bumped and play cards in the loading area until they are notified. They receive their free tickets for a flight to Hawaii to be used sometime later, and return to the ticket window to exchange their original refundable tickets for cash.

These folks visit Hawaii whenever they wish, and they always go free as the guest of an airline which was overbooked and bumped them from their scheduled flight.

Remember that with any of the strategies mentioned in this book, flexibility is the key. In addition, the information you can accumulate by visiting your local airport and talking to personnel is invaluable. As with most endeavors, a little time spent in preparation usually pays big dividends.

Back to Back Tickets

In the discussion of airline pricing it was mentioned that unless you stay through a weekend (usually a seven-day stay with a Saturday night stay-over), you aren't eligible for the special promotional or excursion fare. Well, the "back to back" strategy is a way to work around this particular restriction. This strategy (sometimes called "nested fares"), has several variations and involves some pre-planning, but is of particular value for business travelers who can't meet the airlines' promotional restrictions. Here are several of the variations.

■ BASIC BACK TO BACK

Let's say you have to leave Seattle for New York on Tuesday, the 1st, and must return by Friday, the 4th. You won't be staying seven days or over Saturday night, so you don't qualify for a promotional fare. The full round-trip fare from Seattle to New York is $1,702.

Instead of purchasing the full fare round trip tickets leaving Seattle on the 1st and returning from New York on the 4th, buy two promotional round-trip tickets. Ticket #1 leaves Seattle for New York on the 1st with a return date based on the requirements. Ticket #2 is a New York-Seattle round-trip leaving New York on the 4th, meeting the same airline requirements.

You will use the top coupon on ticket #1 for your flight to New York and the top coupon on ticket #2 for your return to Seattle on the 4th. Each of these promotional round-trip tickets cost $289 for a total cost of $578. The overall savings on the Seattle to New York trip are $1,124. The bottom or second coupon on each ticket is either throw away or sold by classified advertising.

Keep in mind that you don't buy two Seattle/New York round-trip tickets. If you did, you would be using the top coupon for Seattle-New York to get there and would need to use the second coupon of ticket #2 to return. The airline computer system would pick up the fact that you failed to use the top coupon (Seattle-New York) and would automatically cancel the return coupon assuming that you failed to make the trip. When using this strategy make sure it is always the bottom or return coupon that is discarded or resold.

This is an excellent strategy for businesses that are frequently sending employees across the country to certain cities. One employee uses the top ticket to get to a destination and another employee uses 2nd coupon to return. That way the business always gets the benefit of the promotional fare. One last consideration for the business and the employee - whose name is on which ticket?

Keep in mind that although your travel agent may be very conscientious and try to get you the best available airfares, they receive their commissions from the airlines. Worries about airline retaliation may prevent some travel agents from selling both back-to-back tickets. Depending upon your relationship with your travel agent, you may want to buy each of the tickets from a different agent. If you go through all the effort to purchase each ticket from a different travel agent, you may want to book each flight on a different airline.

■ BUDGET BACK TO BACK

The "budget back to back" requires a little more research, but uses a booking procedure known as "open-jaws" to provide additional savings. The idea here is that since I'm not going to use the 2nd coupon on each ticket, why not try to increase my savings on its purchase. To do this you book an "open-jaws" ticket.

The term "open-jaws" is used to describe a trip where the passenger flies into one city and returns from another. It derives from the fact that if you drew a straight line to and from the different cities, you would have a triangle resembling an animal's open jaws. Airlines allow passengers to book "open-jaws" excursion fares with only one additional requirement. The new restriction states that the "open-jaws" distance from city to city must be the shortest leg in the triangle.

Here's how you can use this fact to your advantage. Instead of simply booking ticket #1 SEA/NY/SEA and ticket #2 NY/SEA/NY, you will try to get a real bargain on the last leg of both tickets. The last leg of each ticket (the throwaway portion) will be the "open jaw."

You check with your travel agent or use the Internet to locate a city with a better return fare, and book the 2nd coupon of the return from that location. You find that you can save an additional $50 if you return from Dulles International Airport in VA, rather than Kennedy Airport in NY. You also locate a great fare out of San Francisco, for your return from Seattle. By using this additional strategy, you save an additional $100, and now your savings over the $1702 round-trip ticket to New York are $1,206, or 70%.

Your final booking looks like this:

- Ticket #1   Seattle/NY/Dulles/Seattle
- Ticket #2   NY/Seattle/San Francisco/NY

■ BACK TO BACK FULL UTILIZATION

Let's go back to our previous example. You know you have to make a business trip from Seattle to New York leaving Seattle on Tuesday, the 1st, and returning from New York on Friday, the 4th. You like the idea of the basic "back to back" strategy, but your a penny-pincher and deplore the idea of discarding these two bottom coupons of my tickets. Isn't there some way you can use them?

Well, you happen to know that later in the year, you need to make this same trip again, on business, but you don't know the specific dates. Your next trip might be necessary in two months, or you might not need to repeat the trip for another eight months. No problem. How about this solution? When you purchase each of these two tickets, you allow yourself maximum leeway for the future.

- Ticket #1 is a Seattle to New York round-trip leaving on Tuesday, July 1st, and returning on a weekday nine months from your departure date. This ticket is booked with an open return date to be specified later.
- Ticket #2 is a New York to Seattle round-trip leaving New York on the 4th and returning from Seattle again with an open return date.

When you learn the specifics of your later trip, you arrange the exact date on both tickets so that ticket #2 has a return date a few days earlier than ticket #1. You then use ticket #2 to travel to New York, and ticket #1 to return to Seattle a few days later.

■ HIDDEN CITY BACK TO BACK

Here's a strategy you can employ if you know you don't have any plans to return a second time to the destination city. Use the hidden city strategy (described later in this book) to increase your savings.

After you have used the lower cost hidden city round-trip to get to your destination, you can then buy your second round-trip from your actual destination and use coupon #1 to return home. It might give you some additional savings to use a one-way return to an alternate city. As with any strategy described in Part II of this book, never overlook the possibility of using an upstart or low-cost carrier for a one-way return.

■ BACK TO BACK OPEN JAWS

Here's a variation of the fully utilized "back to back" you can use if your planning two trips east this year from Seattle. First you need to visit New York on a short trip, and then later in the year you need to be in Washington D.C. for two days. By now I'm assuming you are thinking ahead and understand how to book this one.

- Ticket #1 is Seattle/NY/Dulles/Seattle
- Ticket #2 is NY/Seattle/Seattle/Dulles

Your first trip takes you from Seattle to New York on the top coupon of ticket #1. You return from New York to Seattle using the top coupon of ticket #2.

Months later this year, your second trip is from Seattle to Washington D.C. (Dulles International Airport, VA) on coupon #2 ticket #2. You then use coupon #2 ticket #1 to return to Seattle from Washington D.C.

This is a great strategy for business people making numerous cross-country trips each year, and with a little advance planning it can be used any number of times to save up to 70% on airfare costs. Large corporations, and often government agencies, use this strategy all the time. Why not begin using it for your business and vacation trips?

■ CAUTION

As I've mentioned throughout this book, airlines become very testy when they discover you have circumvented their pricing rules and regulations. American Airlines takes a particularly stringent stand against anyone using two or more tickets "end to end" to bypass their requirements. Several of the other airlines also have rules against using more than a single ticket. Airline ticket personnel are well aware of this tactic, and are encouraged by the aforementioned airlines to confiscate your ticket if you are discovered using this ploy.

I believe using these strong-arm tactics to perpetuate their predatory pricing policies would never stand up in court, and hope some wealthy traveler will take them to court and settle the matter once and for all. Until that time, the wisest course of action is probably to use the strategy on the airlines that are more concerned with selling you a ticket, rather than embarrassing customers at their ticket windows. I would also remember these names when making airline recommendations to friends. Personally, I refuse to fly on airlines that show no concern for public relations.

The big three, Continental, Delta, and United, have no particular policy against multiple tickets at present, but in the airline business policies are constantly changing, so be aware.

■ SANCTIONED BACK TO BACK

If the idea of employing a tactic the airlines say is against their rules or the risk of an embarrassing confrontation at a ticket window would restrict your use of the "back to back" strategy, here is a method, that is in compliance with the airline rules. You can use "back to back" tickets (any of the given strategies) as long as you buy your tickets from two different airlines. This would bypass any airline rule against use of multiple tickets.

The same is true if you combine a round-trip ticket with a one-way return. The idea here would be to buy a ticket with 3 coupons. Coupon #1 would be a one-way full fare ticket from sea/ny. Coupon #2 and #3 would be a low cost promotional round-trip ticket from ny/sea. Coupon #2 (NY/SEA) would be your return ticket to Seattle. Coupon #3 (SEA/NY) could be used for a later trip to New York, or discarded.

Many travelers use the "back to back" family of strategies all the time, so I've listed some of the common sense precautions they employ.

- Choose the correct airline: Combine the information I've given you with some investigating on your own to select the proper airlines for this strategy.
- Use different travel agents: It makes no sense to get your favorite travel agent in trouble over using multiple tickets. Theoretically an airline could refuse business to any agent they felt was assisting customers in efforts to circumvent their rules. Your travel agent can be your best friend in procuring travel bargains, so why put them in jeopardy.
- Use different airlines: It makes sense to use two or more different airlines when using any multiple ticket strategy. Your transaction is not apt to be detected on any single airline computer system.
- Book your tickets on different days: Once again this removes the opportunity of some reservationist discovering your strategy.
- Use discretion: Never inform other passengers that you are using a strategy. Never let anyone see more than one ticket. Always keep your tickets separate and intact. Never throw away a second coupon before you have used the first coupon. Always present the proper tickets when attempting to change the second coupon or boarding the aircraft.
- Be polite and use common sense:

By using these simple precautions, you can be one of the many bargain conscious travelers using the "back to back" strategy to save up to 70% on your future airfares.

Frequent Flyers

 Many polls of travelers have shown that one of their major concerns when purchasing airline tickets are the airlines' Frequent Flyer programs. Often this consideration is given more importance than the actual fare. A little mathematical calculation will show that a frequent flyer award is valued at two cents a mile. Keeping this fact in mind, it doesn't make much sense to me to use this criterion to select which airline you will fly. Savings obtained through most of the other strategies mentioned in this book will usually result in much greater savings. In addition, only about 15 % of frequent flyer awards are ever actually redeemed for tickets.

Realizing that the frequent flyer programs are an airlines promotional ploy to develop loyalty, not a way to give passengers bargain airfares, let's look at some of the plans and their provisions.

Soon after American Airlines launched the first frequent flyer promotion in 1981, other airlines began to initiate their own programs. The program became popular immediately, and is generally considered the single greatest airline promotion in history. Americans alone hold over two trillion miles of frequent flyer awards. Since their introduction, the airlines have added several restrictions such as "blackout dates" (periods of time when you are unable to use them), and expiration dates at which time (usually three years), they become worthless. The total number of miles needed before you can redeem them for a flight credit has also been raised. Even with these changing restrictions, they continue to be among the airlines most popular promotions.

Most of the major airlines now have credit cards and will award you a frequent flyer mile for every dollar charged on their card. These cards usually carry high annual interest rates, so they are, at best, a dubious bargain. Unless you pay off your credit card balance every month, the awards are more than offset by the high interest rates.

Some banks have offered frequent flyer miles as a reward for using their credit cards. AT&T, Sprint, MCI, and a host of other telephone companies also award frequent flyer miles on certain affiliated airlines. The frequent flyer craze has so permeated our society that they have become a type of currency and are offered for everything from department store purchases to magazine subscriptions.

Northwest Airlines launched a restaurant awards program in 1993, and most airlines now have a "dining awards" program. United's several restaurant programs now include over *10,000* establishments. Most of the participating airlines offer two to five miles per dollar spent in the dining program. Needless to say, this program has been very successful among business travelers who "wine and dine" their clients.

Any program with this degree of popularity was bound to attract some scam artists, and the airlines have begun a major crack down on these fraudulent schemes to amass frequent flyer miles. Some of the most common scams are:

- Purchasing a full-fare refundable ticket, checking in to receive the frequent flyer miles, then redeeming the ticket and not making the flight.
- Paying someone to fly under your name to receive his or her awards.
- Buying someone else's frequent flyer awards.

■ RECOMMENDATIONS

Realizing that these frequent flyer promotions are in a state of constant flux, there are still some general recommendations I would give if you plan to use them to help offset your airfare costs.

- Try to limit yourself to two or three programs, then use other strategies in this book to reduce ticket costs on the selected airlines. Anticipate future destinations and join the program of the appropriate airline.
- Always check the hotel and car rental affiliation of the airlines since these additional awards can add substantially to your mileage total.

- If you are pre-committed to a credit card, check its airline affiliation.
- Check out the partner airlines. TWA honors miles awarded on Aerolineas Argentines, Air India, Philippine Airlines, Alaska Airlines, and Horizon Air. As of this date, Alaska Airlines appears to have partnerships with most major airlines except Delta and United.
- Read all of the program's policies. Are miles transferable to other family members? What level of travel is required for elite membership? What is the particular airline's policy on expiring miles? Continental and Delta have no expiration dates on their frequent flyer awards as long as you make a flight every three years. Southwest and TWA have no expiration date and no flight requirements.
- Will the airline you select grant frequent flyer miles on tickets purchased from consolidators?

■ REDEMPTION HINTS
- Begin trying to redeem for the flight you want one year in advance.
- Try alternate dates and alternate cities if you are unable to get tickets to your original choice.
- Always check seat availability on partner airlines.
- Keep all boarding passes until you receive your statement to make sure the airlines has credited your frequent flyer miles.
- If you are close to your goal, purchase the additional award miles from the airline.
- Call shortly after midnight a few days before your desired departure. Some airlines, like Alaska Airlines, will release unsold seats to frequent flyers a day or two before departure.

■ SAMPLE PROGRAMS
Here are some examples of some major airlines' frequent flyer programs. These examples are not meant to be complete, and only

give partial information. The specifics of these programs are always changing, so contact the individual airline for complete information.

ALASKA AIRLINES MILEAGE PLAN   800-654-5669

Expiration: no expiration

Requirements: 20,000 miles

Partners: British Airways, Horizon Air, Northwest, Quantas, SAS, and TWA

Car Rental: Alamo, Budget, and Hertz

Hotels: Hilton, Holiday Inn, Hyatt, Red Lion, and Westin

Credit Cards: Alaska Airlines, Seafirst Visa, MasterCard, and Diners Club

Phone: AT&T and Sprint

AMERICA WEST FLIGHT FUND   800-247-5691

Expiration: no expiration with flight each 3-year period

Requirements: 20,000 Domestic, 30,000 Hawaiian, 60,000 European

Partner: Aeromexico, America West, and Continental

Car Rental: Avis, Dollar, and Thrifty

Hotels: Hilton, Radisson, Westin, and Holiday Inn

Credit Cards: America West Flight Fund Visa, and Diners Club

Phone: Sprint

AMERICAN AIRLINES AADVANTAGE   800-882-8880

Expiration: Jan. 1, after 3 years

Requirements: 25,000 Domestic, 35,000 Hawaiian, 60,000 European

Partners: American Eagle, Cathay Pacific, Hawaiian, Quantas, Air Pacific, and RenoAir

Car Rental: Thrifty

Hotels: Sheraton, Hyatt, Hilton, Holiday Inn, Marriott, and Red Lion

Credit Cards: Citibank AAdvantage Card, and Diners Club

Phone: MCI

CONTINENTAL ONEPASS   713-952-1630

Expiration: no expiration with flight each *3* years

Requirements: 25,000 Domestic, 45,000 Hawaiian, 50,000 European

Partners: Aerolinas Argentina, Air Canada, America West, Quantas, and SAS

Car Rental: Avis, Hertz, National, and Thrifty

Hotels: Fiesta Inns, Marriott, Radisson, and Sheraton

Credit Cards: Chase/Continental Bank Card, MasterCard, and Diners Club

Phone: MCI

DELTA SKYMILES   800-323-2323

Expiration: no expiration with flight each 3 years

Requirements: 25,000 Domestic, 30,000 Hawaiian, 50,000 European

Partners: Air New Zealand, Aeromexico, Finnair, SwissAir, and Varig

Car Rental: Alamo, Avis, and Hertz

Hotels: Holiday Inns, Hilton, Hyatt, Marriot, and Radisson

Credit Cards: Delta Skymiles, American Express

Phone: MCI

NORTHWEST WORLDPASS   800-447-3757

Expiration: Jan. 1, of year 3

Requirements: 25,000 Domestic, 40,000 Hawaiian, 35,000 European

Partners: Air UK, Alaska Airlines, America West, Horizon, KLM, and US Air

Car Rental: Alamo, Avis, Hertz, Budget, and National

Hotels: Holiday Inns, Hyatt, Hilton, Marriott, and Radisson

Credit Cards: Northwest WorldPass Visa, and Diners Club

Phone: MCI

SOUTHWEST RAPID REWARDS   800-445-5764

Expiration: Credits expire 1 year from 1 st flight

Requirements: 16 Credits equal one round-trip

Partners: none

Car Rentals: Dollar Rent A Car

Credit Cards: Southwest Airlines Rapid Rewards Visa, and Diners Club

Phone: MCI

TWA FREQUENT FLIGHT BONUS   800-325-4815

Expiration: no expiration

Requirements: 20,000 Domestic, 40,000 Hawaiian, 35,000 European

Partners: Aerolinas Argentina, Alaska Airlines, and Horizon Air

Car Rental: Avis, Alamo, and Thrifty

Hotels: Hilton, Marriott, Radisson, and Forte

Credit Cards: TWA Getaway, EAB Visa, and Diners Club

Phone: Sprint

HAWAIIAN HAWAIIANMILES   800-367-7637

Expiration: no expiration with flight each 3-year period

Requirements: 5,000 equals a one way inter-island ticket

Partners: none

Car Rental: Avis and Alamo

Hotels: Aston, Castle Resorts, Hawaiian Pacific Resorts, and Village Resorts

Credit Cards: American Express, MasterCard, and Diners Club

UNITED MILEAGE PLUS   605-399-2400

Expiration: Jan. 1 of year 3

Requirements: 25,000 Domestic, 35,000 Hawaiian, 50,000 European

Partners: Air Canada, Air France, Aloha, and Amsett

Car Rental: Alamo, Avis, Budget, Dollar, Hertz, and National

Hotels: Holiday Inns, Hyatt, Sheraton, Hilton, and Westin

Credit Cards: United Mileage Plus Visa, and Diners Club

Phone: MCI

USAIR FREQUENT TRAVELER   800-872-4738

Expiration: no expiration

Requirements: 25,000 Domestic, 40,000 European

Partners: Air France, British Airways, Northwest, Quantas, MetroJet, and SwissAir

Car Rental: Alamo, Avis, Hertz, and National

Hotels: Hilton, Hyatt, Marriott, Radisson, and Westin

Credit Cards: USAir/Nationsbank Visa, and Diners Club

Phone: MCI

If you are interested in the latest information on frequent flyer programs here is the monthly publication for you. A yearly subscription is $36.

INSIDE FLYER
4715-C Town Center Drive
Colorado Springs, CO 80916-4709
719-597-8880
www.insideflyer.com

Hidden City

If you are beginning to become knowledgeable about bargain airfare tickets, here's a tactic that may have crossed your mind. Although I normally don't endorse this strategy, you will probably come across it sooner or later, so I will include it in the book for the sake of thoroughness. The airlines hate this one, and have strict rules in force in attempts to block its use. However, some creative travelers still employ this strategy in an attempt to circumvent the airlines' pricing schedules. Often it can lead to savings of up to 75%.

There was a time when travel agents, and the airlines themselves, engaged in "point beyond" ticketing. The Civil Aeronautics Board (CAB) even endorsed the practice realizing the inequity of allowing passengers to fly farther for less then the fare paid by those who deplane at a stopover. The agents or airlines simply used the cheaper "point beyond" to calculate the ticket price. At the time, some airlines even offered advice on using this strategy.

After airline deregulation, this all changed. With the increased competition, the airlines began to place much more importance on their bottom line. Given a choice between customer satisfaction and profits, the airlines deferred to their accounting departments, and any concern with assisting a passenger seeking the lowest possible fare was eliminated.

Most of the major airlines set a minimum and maximum length of stay requirement if you want to receive discounted fares. These requirements vary, but usually stipulate a 7-day stay over a Saturday night. These requirements are usually in addition to the 30-day advance purchase requirements explained in the section of this book dealing with APEX fares. These restrictions are in place to require most business travelers to purchase more expensive fares, since they usually can't meet the requirements. Often business travelers will use the "hidden city" strategy in an attempt to avoid paying this penalty fare. Here's how it works.

Airline ticket fares are based upon traffic and competition, not distance traveled. Often a ticket to a city far beyond your destination is cheaper than a fare to your intended airport. If you've read some of the previous strategies in this book, an alarm probably just went off in your head. You're becoming more knowledgeable and beginning to use that knowledge to see some possibilities. This all leads us to the "hidden city" or "point-beyond" ticketing strategy.

Let's say you need to complete a last minute trip to Houston. You check on a last minute one-way from Seattle to Houston and find the best fare is $781. While your checking, you notice that you can get a last minute flight from Seattle to Orlando (lots of competition on those tickets to Walt Disney World) for $540. You also notice the Orlando flight has a stopover in Houston. You buy the Orlando ticket, save *$241*, and deplane in Houston.

Obviously this strategy is not designed for passengers with a lot of baggage to check. As I've discussed other places in the book, always travel with only carry-on luggage if possible. Learning the skill of limiting yourself to carry-on baggage is invaluable.

At this point I can hear you saying to yourself, "This sounds like it might work okay with one-way tickets, but can you use it to make round-trips? " See if you can follow this example.

You live near Atlanta, and you need to make a quick round-trip to Pittsburgh. Your not sure when you will return from Pittsburgh, but you know it will just be a day or two, and you will not be staying through the weekend. You check on a round-trip ticket to leave in the morning and see that the price is $980. Instead, you buy the following tickets at two different travel agencies.

Your first ticket is a one-way ticket from Atlanta to Youngstown, and contains two coupons. The top coupon takes you from Atlanta to a stopover in Pittsburgh where you deplane. The second coupon was for travel from Pittsburgh to Youngstown, and is not used.

Ticket number two is a one-way ticket from Pittsburgh, to Birmingham, and also contains two coupons. The top coupon is for travel from Pittsburgh to Atlanta where you deplane. The second coupon was for travel from Atlanta to Birmingham and again goes unused.

Ticket #1 costs $330, and ticket #2 costs $320. The total cost of both tickets is $650, a saving of $330 over the round trip ticket.

To use this strategy you must always plan so that the ticket you use is the top coupon. If you were attempting to use the 2nd coupon of the ticket, the airlines would be alerted by their computer system to the fact that you had not arrived on the 1st coupon's flight. This could prompt the ticket agent to confiscate your ticket, or at the very least, lead to a very unpleasant conversation at the loading gate.

To locate hidden cities, simply pick up a given airlines flight path map and check out their hubs. Anytime you are flying to a hub, it may be possible to locate a city beyond the hub with a better fare. Simply book your flight to the city beyond and deplane at your true destination.

As I've already mentioned, airlines hate this strategy. They are definitely not pleased when they see people bypassing their fare structure. For this reason, this is not a strategy you would discuss with your travel agent. Travel agents are paid a commission by the airlines, and it's not in their self-interest to help you bypass the airlines' restrictions.

I've already revealed that this is not a strategy I normally use or endorse. I have no problem whatsoever bypassing airline rules as long as my actions don't break the law. Most of the strategies in this book are attempts to find ways to avoid paying full fare to the airlines. However, my objection to use of the "hidden city" ploy rests upon security and common courtesy to other passengers.

In these extremely security conscious times, all airport and aircraft employees are watchful for any unexpected changes in routine. Assume for a moment that your flight attendant has taken a count from the aircraft manifest and knows that 20 people will deplane in Chicago before the aircraft leaves for New York. You use the "hidden city" and deplane although you were traveling on a ticket to New York. The flight attendants take their count and notice that one or two extra people have deplaned. What do you think will be on flight crew's mind?

Of course, they will wonder if someone had an explosive device in their luggage and left the plane before it was set to detonate. This could lead to the plane returning to the gate with all baggage to be removed and rechecked. This could involve delays of hours for the remaining passengers. I believe it's possible to locate great bargain airfares and still remain a considerate human being. Nobody needs a bargain airfare this badly.

Alternate Airports

The most common and easiest strategy used to save up to 80% on airfares is the use of alternate cities or airports. Very often, changing the destination airport can save you hundreds of dollars. Instead of flying into New York via Kennedy International airport, you may be able to save hundreds of dollars by flying into Newark, NJ. You use the huge savings to employ ground transportation to travel the 14 miles from Newark to New York City.

When looking for alternate cities, always try to locate one served by an upstart or low-cost carrier like Southwest or American West. Use your travel agent or personal computer to test fares to several alternate destinations. The extra time spent searching out these alternates will probably pay off in tremendous savings on your ticket.

If you travel several times a year or are a business traveler, you will probably want to pick up a route map from your favorite low-cost carrier. Use the route map to locate the alternate cities near your destination cities.

Here is a list of some alternate cities and airports near some of the major domestic airline hubs and gateways. Most of the alternate locations are within 100 miles of the major airports.

Destination	Alternates
Atlanta	Birmingham, Chattanooga
Atlantic City	Philadelphia, Newark, Baltimore
Baltimore	Washington Dulles, Washington National
Boston	Providence, Hartford, Manchester
Chicago	Chicago Midway, Milwaukee
Cincinnati	Dayton, Louisville, Indianapolis, Columbus

Cleveland	Akron, Toledo, Columbus, Pittsburgh
Dallas	Dallas Love Field, Oklahoma City, Austin
Denver	Colorado Springs
Detroit	Detroit City Airport, Toronto Windsor
Houston	Houston Hobby, Austin
Kansas City	Omaha
Los Angeles	Ontario, John Wayne Airport, Burbank
Memphis	Little Rock
Miami	Fort Lauderdale/Hollywood International
New Orleans	Baton Rouge, Pensacola
New York	Newark, MacArthur, Stewart, Westchester
Omaha	Des Moines, Kansas City
Orlando	Tampa, Daytona Beach, Jacksonville
Philadelphia	Newark, Baltimore
Phoenix	Tucson
Pittsburgh	Columbus, Akron, Cleveland, Columbus
Portland	Seattle
Sacramento	Oakland, San Francisco, Reno
St. Louis	Indianapolis
San Diego	Orange County, Palm Springs, Long Beach
San Francisco	Oakland International, San Jose International
Seattle	Portland, Vancouver
Tampa	Orlando, Sarasota, Fort Myers
Washington, DC	Washington National, Baltimore

Product Purchase

During the past several years, major airlines have attempted to outdo one another with their promotions. The airlines have formed partnerships with every possible business endeavor to offer $25-$500 off published ticket prices if you purchase a product or use a particular service. Here are a few of the hundreds of recent promotions.

- Purchase a new Volvo and receive a free roundtrip to Europe from one of 22 major U.S. cities. To qualify, you must purchase the vehicle through their European Overseas Delivery Program. You drive the car during your vacation, and then Volvo will ship the vehicle to your local Volvo dealer.

- Associated Grocers food stores in Washington and Oregon offer a promotion that will discount travel on TWA. A $100 food purchase receipt will allow purchase of a TWA round-trip travel certificate. These certificates allow round-trip travel at reduced fares between Seattle or Portland, and specified cities in the East.

- Purchase a Sea Doo jet boat and receive a certificate for a free round-trip on Delta Air Lines.

- Purchase a $60 annual membership in the Pet Care Savings Club, and in addition to the $190 savings on pet food, receive $160 in discounts on American Airlines.

- Purchase the Warner Brothers' video Shiloh and receive a Continental Airlines travel coupon. The coupon is good for discounts of up to $100 on travel between the U.S. and Mexico, the Caribbean, Canada, or South America.

- Brochures available by request at the check-in desk at Howard Johnson Hotels contain a TWA discount travel coupon of up to $100 for use to Honolulu or within the continental U.S.

- Located within the Passport to Houston free tourist guide is a Continental Airlines discount coupon worth $100 on travel between the U.S. and Mexico, the Caribbean, Canada or South America.

- Purchase an American Express Platinum Card ($300 annual fee) and receive a 2-for-1 free companion ticket each time you purchase a round-trip full fare Business Class international ticket.

- Participating Jiffy Lube locations offer a Continental Airlines discount coupon after an oil change. The certificate is good for $125 on round-trips of $800 or more.

- Purchase a Web TV Internet Terminal from your local Magnavox dealer and receive a certificate good for up to $150 off round-trip domestic travel on American Airlines.

- Purchase a Sony BS1 Satellite System ($299) and get a free domestic round-trip on American Airlines.

- Pre-register by calling TWA's Frequent Flight Bonus line at 800-325-4815 and receive 40,000 bonus miles with one Business Class ticket to Europe. These bonus miles can be redeemed for two free domestic round-trip tickets.

Most of these particular offers have probably expired by the time you are reading this book; however, there are an endless supply of these deals and discounts. The examples I have given were meant to give you some indication of the variety of these offers.

Sometimes a business will offer a free vacation airfare if you buy their product during a sale period. This is a very specialized strategy that is only available where you are making major purchases. It might be worth looking into if you are in the market for a new house or car.

No matter where you are going or which airline you choose, deals are available. Without a doubt the best place to locate these bargains is *"Best Fares Magazine."* *Best Fares* is available only on a membership basis. One-year memberships are currently $59.95 per year.

Best Fares

Discount Travel Magazine
P.O. Box 171212
Arlington, TX 76003
800-880-1234

Segments

Often you can get a better fare by connecting two segments to zig-zag to your destination, rather than booking the non-stop. Dividing your trip into two or more segments is often referred to as "split ticketing." If the fare to your final destination seems too steep, always check the pricing of two tickets with an intermediate stop.

Remember the old adage, "There's more than one way to skin a cat." Well, there is also more than one single route to your destination. Some airline routes are very competitive, while others have low traffic volumes and outrageously high fares. Let's take a look and see how we might use this information to our advantage.

What if you take your trip form city A to city B and break it into segments. You might travel from city A to city C (somewhere near city B) on a low-cost carrier, then take the short last leg from city C to city B on another airline with the best fare we can obtain. Check out this example.

Let's say that you want to fly from Minneapolis to Detroit, but haven't had any advance opportunity to line up discount tickets. You need to leave on Tuesday and return on Friday. There's no chance to get one of the promotional fares, and since you won't be staying over Saturday night, you'll be paying a steep fare. Checking the web page of a major carrier, you find that the full fare round-trip ticket from Minneapolis to Detroit is $896. You notice, however, that you can fly from Minneapolis to Chicago's Midway Airport for $149. The final segment of the trip from Midway to Detroit is $174. Your total cost for the trip is $323 ($149+$174). Your savings over the full fare ticket are $573.

With these colossal savings available, I can't imagine anyone not checking on segments before purchasing full-fare.

Las Vegas is a very popular destination and the airlines regularly offer special fares to fly gamblers into town. Why not use this information to save on any trip to California from the East? How? Well, why not fly into Las Vegas and then take a low-cost carrier like Southwest Airlines for the final leg into San Diego or Los Angeles? Let's look at an example.

Using an Internet flight information system (I used lowestfare.com), I find that a last minute weekday round-trip, from Atlanta to Los Angeles, is $1292. By simply switching the destination city to Las Vegas the fare drops to $493. A connecting round-trip from Las Vegas to Los Angeles on Southwest Airlines is another $ 98. The total price for this round-trip using the segments is $591, less than half the price of the trip as originally planned. Would you use segments to save $701 on this trip?

Recently, a friend of mine needed to take a mid-week trip from Seattle to Miami and return in two days. He needed to leave on a Tuesday and return on Thursday evening. It was already Sunday evening when we started looking at the fares. The last minute round-trip fare economy fare to Miami was $1189.

Once again using the Internet, we booked the following segments. The first ticket was a round-trip to Orlando. Since Walt Disney World is located in Orlando, often you can locate reasonably priced tickets designed to promote this attraction. We were able to purchase the round-trip for $471. We then added an Orlando to Miami round-trip segment on Gulfstream (a Florida area low-cost carrier) for $190. The total fare for our Seattle to Miami round-trip using segments was $661. The total savings, using segments, was $1189-$661 = $528.

Here are a few things to look for if you hope to use this strategy. The flights to major airline hubs (St. Louis, Atlanta, Chicago, Denver, and Las Vegas) are usually very competitive. Always look for a way to use them. If you are planning a trip to Walt Disney World at Orlando, can you use Atlanta? If you are planning a trip to Portland or Seattle, you might want to look at Denver or Las Vegas.

Another thing to keep in mind is the amount of baggage accompanying you on your journey. Split ticketing usually (but not always) involves flights on two or more different airlines. This can be a real headache if you are traveling with checked baggage. If you do have to travel with a volume of baggage, simply overnight ship your luggage to your hotel. The savings on the split ticketing examples I have given will more than pay for the overnight shipment.

Most veteran travelers always try to get by with carry-on baggage. In 1996, my daughter and I took a 23-day tour of Europe using only carry-on luggage. There is no greater feeling than flying into a major airport, walking directly to the car rental, driving to your hotel, sitting on your bed, and realizing that many of your flight companions are still circling the baggage carrousel.

Companion/Discounts

■ COMPANION FARES

Companion, or two-for-one fares, have become the most popular of all airline promotions with the exception of the Frequent Flyer programs. These companion tickets can be a substantial bargain, since the two individuals traveling divide the price of the ticket. However, there are often several drawbacks.

- Both individuals must travel the same segments on the same airlines at the same time.
- Often they are very restrictive in terms of blackout periods.
- Usually you will have to purchase a higher-priced ticket based upon a published fare. After reading this book you should be expecting to locate a ticket at a 40% discount from published fares. Be sure you do the math.

HERE ARE SOME RECENT EXAMPLES:

- Continental offers a $99 companion ticket to new members of their OnePass program.
- Purchase an Alaska Airlines Platinum Visa card from Bank of America and earn a $50 companion roundtrip. You also receive 5000 bonus Mileage Plan miles and other benefits.
- Starwood Vacations' *Second Person Flies Free to Hawaii* promotion provides free companion air travel to one of five Hawaiian Islands with the purchase of seven hotel nights at your choice of 15 locations. Travel is from the mainland U.S. via Continental, Delta or United.
- Pay the published rack rate for an overnight stay at Fairmont Hotels and receive a $99 American Airlines companion ticket good for travel in the continental U.S.

- Delta Airlines and American Express are offering a free companion roundtrip certificate each year upon renewal of their co-branded Platinum Delta SkyMiles Credit Card.

■ DISCOUNT CERTIFICATES

Discount certificate offers usually have time limitations. Here are some recent examples:

- Receive over $500 of discounts on air travel and hotels by using the coupon on the back Dove ice cream bars.
- Receive a discount certificate for up to $250 off Continental airfares by purchasing special Warner Brothers videos.
- Purchase MapQuest's USA 99: *Streets & Destinations CD*, and receive four Continental coupons with a value to $1,900.
- Sears Discount Travel Club is offering new members certificates valued to $700 for travel on American Airlines.
- Stay one night at a participating Westin Hotel, receive a 20-40% discount, and get a booklet that contains coupons for up to $250 off on Continental Airlines travel.

Without a doubt the best place to locate timely information on Companion Fares, discount certificates, and vacation package bargains is *Best Fares Magazine. Best Fares* is available only on a membership basis. One-year memberships are currently $59.95 per year.

Best Fares

Discount Travel Magazine
P.O. Box 171212
Arlington, TX 76003
800-880-1234

Fare Wars

You are already probably aware of this option. Flexibility is the key here. If you have the ability to wait for the inevitable airline price war before taking your vacation or trip, you can travel at a fraction of the cost of a full fare. Be ready. Only a limited number of seats on a flight to any specific location will be offered at the cut-rate, so these tickets are sold on a first come, first serve, basis. Once again, be prepared. Here are some hints for making the most of fare war opportunities.

- Be vigilant. Fare wars seem to occur about four to six times each year. International fare wars are more common to the airlines serving Europe than any other destinations. If you are planning a trip, especially to Europe, check your local paper's business section each day. If a major fare war begins, even the evening television news programs will mention the sale.

- Act quickly—but not too quickly. Fare wares are a result of the airline management personnel attempting to give sales a boost. They will usually announce their sale at the beginning of the week. These sale prices are on a limited number of seats on selected flights. If other airlines are going to match or beat the sale prices, they will act within a day or two. Sometimes it pays to wait a day or so until the prices are set, however, if you wait too long you could find it nearly impossible to locate a ticket.

- The best strategy is to reserve a seat quickly, as soon as the fare war is announced. Use the reservation as a backup while you continue to investigate the possibility of a better fare from another airline attempting to match or beat the sale prices. Be sure to ask your travel agent if they will cancel your original ticket and reissue a ticket at a lower fare if you locate one. Your agent may do this at no cost, but more likely will charge you a change fee.

- Be aware. Although the airlines always advertise that they will honor a new fare if prices are reduced during a fare war, they seldom mention the $50 processing fee to change the ticket.

- Don't waste a promotional coupon or discount certificate by purchasing too soon or you will cancel out any savings you could have obtained by waiting to use them during the fare war. If you plan your trip far enough in advance, you will almost always have the opportunity to purchase tickets at fare war prices.

- Airlines usually update their computer fare schedules three times a day. If an airline is going to begin a fare war, they often will begin the new rate on their last daily posting at 8 p.m. This gives them a 12-hour lead time advantage over their competition. If you hear rumors of an impending fare war, check the rate schedule after 8 p.m. on Sunday evening.

- Always use the other strategies you have learned and do not simply assume that a ticket during a fare war is the lowest possible price on any given ticket.

World Tour

Although not technically a bargain tactic, if you have grand vacation plans, an "around-the-world" booking can offer incredible savings. Most domestic U.S. Airlines offer around the world fares in conjunction with their worldwide affiliates. If you book your flight through one of these airlines, you are allowed a specific number of stopovers during a specific time frame.

■ RTW BASICS

Pan American Airlines popularized the Around-the-World (RTW) single-fare concept in the 1960's. Currently no airline other than United can claim to "fly around the world." This fact means that in order to offer a one fare RTW, airlines have formed certain alliances or partnerships.

Once you begin your trip, you are required to continue in the same general eastward or westward direction. Backtracking or returning to a previously visited city is not allowed. You are only allowed to cross the Pacific and Atlantic Oceans once on the RTW ticket. Often certain European airlines will allow an exception to this rule by permitting trips back through their hubs. This gives you some flexibility for off-route side-trips.

Normally you are required to purchase RTW tickets 21 days in advance. Most airlines will allow changes to your itinerary. Substantial discounts (50-70%) are available for children ages 2-11.

You are, however, usually allowed to make as many stops as you like, as long as they are on the path of your travel eastward or westward, and are reached by an airline that is a participating partner on your itinerary. Particularly in Asia, there are some either-or choices that must be made. With the development of long-range aircraft, it is increasingly difficult to plan short-haul stopovers.

RTW airlines, and their partners, base their fares on two different concepts. The traditional routing plan was based on the "loop" formula. Your trip was based on a continuous path, or loop, returning to your departure point. Some travel to "off-loop" cities was allowed as long as you continued in the same general direction.

In recent years, many airlines and their partners have begun to use a mileage-based model. The airlines are not concerned if your travel is off-loop; your ticket simply specifies a maximum allowable mileage. When you purchase your ticket, you select a mileage plan that fits your desired itinerary. This allows much more flexibility for backtracking. You will still normally be limited one stop at each city.

■ RTW ROUTINGS

When you decide to book a RTW, you will need to choose from one of three possible routings.

Northern: This is a routing across the North Pacific, across Asia, on to Europe, and home across the Atlantic.. Usually this will allow a stop in Hawaii if you wish.

Southern: This option crosses the South Pacific. The possible additions here include Australia, Fiji, New Zealand, Cook Islands, and other South Pacific islands. With the exception of this South Pacific loop, this routing is identical to the northern routing.

Southern Hemisphere: There are a few airline partnerships that provide a Southern Hemisphere option. This routing typically includes South America, South Africa, New Zealand, and Southeast Asia. Flights cross the South Pacific, Indian Ocean, and South Atlantic.

■ RTW PRICING

According to a recent article in *Consumer Reports Travel Letter*—a must read if you are contemplating a RTW—prices of RTW's can provide exceptional bargains (40-50%) for those traveling in Business Class. Economy RTW fares are usually higher than APEX rates. For this reason, always investigate the possibility of creating your own RTW by combining a series of individual consolidator tickets between the destinations of your choice.

My personal favorite among the discount agencies is High Adventure Travel. Use their Web site (www.airtreks.com) to construct your own custom RTW.

If an RTW is in your future, you will want to locate the August 1998 issue of *Consumer Reports Travel Letter*. Back issues are available. Yearly subscriptions are $39.

Consumer Reports Travel Letter
Subscription Department
P.O. Box 51366
Boulder, CO 80323-1366

One of the more prominent RTW agencies is Air Brokers International. They offer the following guidelines:

- Most travel should be in one continuous direction.
- The fewer carriers used, the greater the savings.
- You can start and end in any U.S. gateway.
- Travel into the Southern Hemisphere increases costs.
- If Europe is involved in your itinerary, it is customary to fly into one European city and out of another.
- Children's fares are usually at a reduced rate.

Air Brokers International, Inc
150 Post Street Suite 620
San Francisco, CA 94108
1-800-883-3273

■ EXAMPLES

Here are some sample itineraries from Air Brokers International's summer 1999 Web site.

$1899   Seattle - Tokyo - Peking - Bangkok - Cairo - Paris - overland to London - Seattle

$1899   Seattle - Tahiti - Auckland - overland to Christchurch - Sydney - Singapore - Bangkok -Hongkong - Seattle

$1999   San Francisco - London - Rome - Delhi - Bangkok - Hongkong - San Francisco

$1849	Los Angeles - Hawaii - Cook Islands - Auckland - Sydney or Brisbane - Bali - Bangkok - Hongkong - Los Angeles
$1899	Los Angeles - Tahiti - Fiji - Auckland - overland to Christchurch - Melbourne - Singapore - overland to Bangkok - Delhi - Rome or Paris or Frankfurt - overland to London - Los Angeles
$1999	Miami - Fiji - Sydney or Melbourne - Singapore - overland to Bangkok - Madrid - overland to London - Miami
$1899	New York - Tokyo - Peking - Bangkok - Athens - Paris - overland to London - New York
$1799	Denver - London - Madrid - Bangkok - overland to Singapore - Bali - Hongkong - Denver
$2249	Chicago - Hongkong - Bangkok - Kuala Lumpur - Capetown - overland to Johannesberg - Harare -Nairobi - Athens or Rome - overland to London - Chicago

Keep in mind that if you are willing to use a consolidator and put the individual segments of the trip together yourself, you may be able to save even more. Be sure to check with a consolidator experienced in putting these segments together. My personal favorite is High Adventure Travel.

High Adventure Travel, Inc.

442 Post Street, 4th Floor
San Francisco, California 94102
Tel: (415)-912-5600
Fax: (415)-912-5606
E-mail: travel@airtreks.com
URL: http://www.airtreks.com

High Adventure Travel's service is called AirTreks.com. Here is some information from their Web site in 1999.

Around-the-World for $1,200 and up? How do you do it? We scour the globe looking for the best prices on flights and segments between hundreds of destinations around the world. And when we find the best fares, we buy air tickets in bulk. Then we pass the savings on to you.

When you buy an Around-the-World or Circle-Pacific ticket from AirTreks.com, you're tapping into a global network of hundreds of air travel experts. Our unique combination of expert advice and easy-to-use Internet tools make planning an Around-the-World trip and purchasing a ticket simple and fun.

With AirTreks.com, you can create the trip of your lifetime in five easy steps. First, you'll need to decide on your departure point and come up with a list of destinations you would like to visit. Next, use our easy-to-use Internet tools to explore your routing and price options.

Once you've decided on a routing, you'll need to work with an AirTreks.com travel consultant to refine and optimize your itinerary. We'll also let you know exactly what the price for your trip will be. Then we'll check availability and help you reserve seats. Once you're completely satisfied with your dream trip, we'll ask for your payment, order your tickets, and you'll be off!

Don't see something you like? Try TripBuilder to create your own itinerary, or use TripSearch to find a routing that matches your specific criteria.

■ EXAMPLES

Here are some sample itineraries from AirTreks.com's summer 1999 Web site.

WEST COAST

$1200	Los Angeles - Tokyo - Bandar Seri Begawan (Brunei) - Singapore - Kuala Lumpur - Bangkok - Hong Kong - Los Angeles
$1220	San Francisco - Hong Kong - Bangkok - Singapore - Jakarta - Denpasar (Bali) - Los Angeles
$1220	Los Angeles - Hong Kong - Bangkok - Singapore - Jakarta - Denpasar (Bali) - Los Angeles
$1260	San Francisco - London - Hong Kong - San Francisco
$1310	Los Angeles - Seoul - Hong Kong - London - Los Angeles

$1360	Los Angeles - Papeete (Tahiti) - Auckland - Apia (West Samoa) - Honolulu - Los Angeles
$1380	Los Angeles - Taipei - Bangkok - Kathmandu - Paris - Los Angeles
$1560	Los Angeles - Paris - Ho Chi Minh (Saigon) - Hong Kong - Los Angeles
$1710	Los Angeles - Auckland - Brisbane - Bangkok - Taipei - Los Angeles
$1730	Los Angeles - Singapore - Auckland - Nadi (Fiji) - Rarotonga (Cooks) - Papeete (Tahiti) - Los Angeles

EAST COAST

$1320	New York - Hong Kong - Bangkok - Kathmandu London - New York
$1360	New York - Hong Kong - Bangkok - Delhi - Bombay - Paris / Overland on your own / Amsterdam - New York
$1370	New York - London - Hong Kong - Los Angeles - New York
$1400	New York - Bangkok - Kathmandu - London - New York
$1400	New York - Taipei - Hong Kong - Beijing - New York
$1830	New York - Los Angeles - Tokyo - Hong Kong - Bangkok - Kathmandu - Paris - New York
$1900	New York - Taipei - Singapore - Jakarta / Overland on your own / Manila - Ho Chi Minh (Saigon) - Hong Kong - Los Angeles - New York
$1970	New York - Amsterdam / Overland on your own / Paris - Ho Chi Minh (Saigon) / Overland on your own / Bangkok - Bandar Seri Begawan (Brunei) - Perth / Overland on your own / Melbourne - Auckland - Nadi (Fiji) - Papeete (Tahiti) - Los Angeles
$1980	New York - Hong Kong - Singapore - Kuala Lumpur - Manila - Ho Chi Minh (Saigon) - Bangkok - Taipei - New York

■ ADDITIONAL RESOURCES

Around The World Travel
1411 Fourth Ave., Suite 430
Seattle, WA 98101 USA
(800) 766-3601 or (206) 223-3600
URL: http://www.netfare.net

Around the World Travel has been in business for over 10 years and specialize in ATW (RTW) fares. Here are some additional sources to investigate.

World Travellers' Club ©
1475 Polk Street, Level 2
Phone (800) 693-0411
San Francisco, CA 94109
Fax (415) 447-7428
E-Mail: info@around-the-world.com
URL: http://www.around-the-world.com

DIA World Tours
2141 Wisconsin Avenue, N.W.
Washington, D.C. 20007-2232
800-342-8258
Fax to 202-625-0288
URL: http://www.diatravel.com

Special Status

Most airlines will offer special discounts based upon status. The discounts can range from 20% to over 50% depending upon the airline, the destination, and the special status. Some of the special status groups include active-duty military, college students, children, members of a family flying together, senior citizens, or people attending conventions.

To qualify for military or college student discounts, always have the proper documentation. Some airlines also offer "youth fares" to passengers age 12-22. Meeting fares can represent substantial savings, but usually require at least 100 passengers to be attending the meeting or convention. American Airlines recently offered discounted fares for groups of 10 or more traveling together.

Senior citizens age 6 2 and older should investigate the airlines' senior discount coupon books. Each coupon book has a number of coupons entitling the bearer to one-way travel to any of their domestic locations for about $150. TWA recently had a similar coupon program for students age 14-24.

Different airlines have different policies, so always check several sources or talk to a knowledgeable travel agent. At the time of this writing, American, Continental, Delta, Northwest, and United were selling 4 coupon books for $596. These coupons will allow a transcontinental flight for $ 130. This is an astounding value compared to a full fare ticket.

■ SENIOR DISCOUNTS AND STUDENT FARES

Most major U.S. airlines offer books of travel coupons to senior travelers' age 62 or older. For a full discussion of Senior Savings, see that chapter of this book. Students age 12-25 should investigate the Student Identity Card available from the non-profit Council on International Educational Exchange. You can receive their free catalogue at 800-226-8624. For an in-depth discussion of Student Savings, see that chapter of this book.

■ COMPASSION AND BEREAVEMENT FARES

Compassion and Bereavement Fares are negotiated by direct contact with the airlines. These fares can provide discounts of 25-50%. Always be prepared to provide full documentation including relationship to the sick or deceased family member along with phone numbers of physicians and the funeral home.

■ MILITARY FARES

Military fares are available to active duty military and, in certain cases, their dependents. While savings on these tickets are substantial, they usually cost more than an APEX fare so look for the opportunity to use another strategy in combination in order to maximize savings. Combining a military fare with an upstart or low-cost carrier is a natural match. This discount is available for last-minute as well as one-way flights. You will be required to show proper military ID at both the time of ticketing and at check-in.

■ FAMILY FARES

When you are traveling as a family, never overlook the chance of obtaining a family discount. The larger the family, the greater the opportunity for substantial savings. As an example, families flying to Israel are sometimes offered the following special fare. The first child pays full fare. The second child pays 25 % off, while the third child saves 50 %. All additional children receive a 75 % discount. When traveling outside the U.S. always investigate children's fares. Often children age 2-11 are eligible for savings of up to 50 %. No one will offer you a family fare unless you ask, so don't be timid.

Sometimes in an effort to boost sales to a particular location, certain airlines will offer a family special where children can fly free. A recent Southwest Airlines promotion offered free travel to Disneyland for children age 2-11 when accompanying a ticketed adult.

Senior Savings

The major airlines offer four distinct programs for seniors. Age requirements vary—most set the requirement at age 62, the exceptions being United Airlines (age 55) and Southwest Airlines (age 65). Don't settle for the standard discount of 10%. There are some excellent deals available for seniors, but you will have to do some investigating to find the program that is best for you. Here are some details.

■ SENIOR DISCOUNTS (Percentage Discounts)

Most of the major airlines of North America offer a 10% discount to seniors on any of their published fares. Even better, they will give the same discount to a companion of any age who is traveling with a qualifying senior on the same itinerary.

There are a few exceptions to this general policy. Southwest Airlines offers price reductions (discussed later) rather than a straight percentage. As of this date (summer 1999), Midwest Airlines and Reno Air do not allow companion rate reductions.

Of the four programs available to seniors, the 10% discount is the least attractive. These discounts are based on published fares and if you have read the previous chapters of this book you are not likely to be purchasing airline tickets at or near published fares.

■ SENIOR DISCOUNTS (Discounted Fares)

Southwest Airlines offers discounted published fares for seniors age 65 or older. Often it is possible to beat these discounts by simply buying a Southwest APEX type ticket or waiting for a Southwest Internet special to your destination. On routes where other airlines compete with Southwest, they usually match this fare discount. United's Shuttle is another airline offering discounted fares to seniors age 65 or more. There are usually better ways to save on an airline ticket than these meager discounts. Let's look further.

■ SENIOR COUPONS

Here is a program much more attractive than senior discounts and often one of your best bargains for domestic travel—most senior coupons are not currently available for international travel.

Although senior coupons are only valid for 1 year, it is always possible to confirm a trip several months in the future as you approach the end of the redemption period. While a 14-day advance is required, standby status is allowed. Seating is capacity controlled, so booking well in advance is encouraged. A separate coupon book is required for each traveler. This eliminates the possibility of a couple traveling together using coupons from a single coupon book.

You do receive frequent flyer miles, but some airlines (America West, Continental and United) currently impose blackout dates. Since round-trip travel is not required, there are no minimum stay requirements. Airlines will allow you to use connecting flights on a single coupon as long as you do not stop over at a connecting city.

Senior coupons can be a great bargain, particularly for last minute or one-way trips, but you should use them with care. Always check your other options first. Try to never use them on short, domestic trips because there is almost always a cheaper alternative. The coupons are a good deal if your cheapest, low-fare round-trip alternative is $275 or more.

TWA's eight-coupon book ($1,032 or $129 each), in addition to being one of the most economical, also includes a bonus coupon for a 20% discount on European travel. TWA also sells books of companion coupons that can be used by a companion of any age accompanying a senior traveling on a coupon book.

It is essential to check the specifics with an airline before purchasing the coupon books. Check the airline's route map. Does it travel to the locations you are most likely to require? Does the airline allow coupon use to Hawaii, Canada, Mexico, Jamaica, Puerto Rico and the Caribbean? If they do allow travel outside the contiguous 48 states, do they require you to use 2 coupons on each leg of that travel?

For the best up-to-date information on senior airfare coupon booklets check with Travel Companions and ask for the *SeniorFare Bargain Report*. The report is $3.

Jens Jurgen
Travel Companion Exchange
P.O. Box 833-S
Amityville, NY 11701-0833

Here are some specifics of some of the senior coupon plans.

America West Senior Savers
(800) 235-9292
www.americawest.com/senior.htm
- four coupons/$548 ($137 each)
- additional destinations: Vancouver, CA
- two coupons: Anchorage and Mexico
- grandchildren program (may use seniors coupons)
- blackout dates

American Airlines Senior TrAAvler
(800) 237-7981
http://wwwr1.aa.com
- four coupons/$596 ($149 each)
- additional destinations: Puerto Rico and Virgin Islands
- two coupons: Hawaii
- blackout dates

Continental Freedom Trips
(800) 441-1135
www.flycontinental.com/freedom
- four coupons/$579 ($145 each)
- eight coupons/$1,078 ($135 each)
- additional destinations: Caribbean, Mexico, Montreal and Toronto
- two coupons: Alaska and Hawaii
- blackout dates

Delta Young at Heart

(800) 221-1212

http://www.delta-air.com

- four coupons/$596 ($149 each)
- additional destinations: Canada, San Juan and St. Thomas
- two coupons: Alaska and Hawaii
- no blackout dates

Midway Senior Travel Booklet

(800) 446-4392

www.midwayair.com/special.html

- four coupons/$390 ($98 each)
- four companion coupons/$440 ($110 each)
- age 60 eligibility

Northwest NorthBest Senior Travel Coupons

(800) 225-2525

http://www.nwa.com

- four coupons/$560 ($140 each)
- additional destinations: Canada
- two coupons: Alaska and Hawaii
- no blackout dates

TWA Senior Travel Pak

(800) 221-2000

http://www.twa.com/

- four coupons/$548 ($137 each)
- eight coupons/$1,032 ($129 each)
- four companion coupons/$648 ($162 each)
- additional destinations: Jamaica, San Juan, Santo Domingo and Toronto
- two coupons: Hawaii
- blackout dates

United Silver TravelPak

(800) 633-6563

http://www.ual.com

- four coupons/$596 ($149 each)
- additional destinations: Canada and San Juan
- two coupons: Alaska and Hawaii
- single coupon: Seattle to Anchorage or Fairbanks
- blackout dates

US Airways Golden Opportunities

(800) 428-4322

www.usairways.com/travel.fares/sen_trav.htm

- four coupons/$579 ($145 each)
- additional destinations: Canada, Mexico, Puerto Rico, and Virgin Islands
- grandchildren program (may use senior's coupons)

■ SENIOR CLUBS

Senior clubs are one of the few real bargains offered by 4 of the major airlines. If you make more than two round-trips a year and meet the age requirements, be sure to investigate these programs.

American Airlines

AActive American Traveler Club

(800) 421-5600

www.aa.aatc.com

American's travel club is for seniors age 62 and above. Members' benefits include domestic round-trips beginning at $98. International round-trips begin at $198. Exact fares are based on distance zones between city pairs. Throughout your enrollment American sends additional airfare discount offers to its members. Additional benefits include discounts on car rentals, hotel rates, tours and cruise trips.

The enrollment fee is $40, and for an additional $30 you can purchase a companion membership allowing discounted travel for a traveling companion of any age. In addition, you can travel with a different companion each time you travel. Traveling companions must follow the same itinerary.

As with most of the major airline travel clubs, membership is limited to a specific number of members, and enrollment ends when that number is reached. A limited number of seats are available on any given flight and blackout dates are also in effect. Currently membership is open through September 2000.

Continental Airlines
Freedom Flight Club
(800) 248-8996
www.flycontinental.com/freedom
Enrollment in Continental's travel club is also for seniors age 62 and above. Membership fees are $75 for domestic trips and $125 for domestic and international travel. The discounts are available for both Continental and Continental Express.

Discounts are based on travel days. Travel on weekdays and Saturdays receive a 20% discount. Friday and Sunday travel discounts are 15%. Membership is good for 1 year and the discounts are based on published fares. Currently there is no expiration date on enrollment.

Delta Airlines
Sky Wise
(800) 325-3750
www.delta-air.com/SkyWise
Delta's Skywise program is available to travelers age 62 and above. Membership is currently closed (summer 1999), but you can register for their waiting list. Membership is $40, and you can enroll up to three traveling companions of any age for an additional $25 each.

Fares are based on travel zones and vary from $118 to $658. While these trips require a Saturday night stay-over, there are currently no blackout dates.

United Airlines
Silver Wings Plus
(800) 720-1765
www.silverwingsplus.com
Here is my personal favorite. United's program is open to seniors age 55 and above. This liberal age requirement makes it available to many business travelers. This travel club has a variety of benefits

for its members. There are travel-zoned fares similar to the other travel clubs, but there are also occasional special offers that provide exceptional savings. The membership fee is $75 for a two-year membership, and $225 for a lifetime enrollment.

Some of the membership benefits include:

- Special offers and periodic discounts for roundtrip travel in the U.S., Canada, and Puerto Rico for as little as $98.
- Special offers from United Airlines partners around the world.
- 50% discounts from participating Sheraton and Hilton Hotels and Resorts.
- Special savings on some of the world's leading cruise lines.
- Discounts and upgrades from car rental companies.

If you become a lifetime member, you also receive new member travel certificates worth over $2,500. United also gives you membership in their On-Call Vacations travel program with outstanding savings on last-minute vacation packages. These savings often can reach 70% on selected cruises.

■ INTERNATIONAL OFFERS
Most international airlines offer a 10% discount to senior travelers and their companions. A few airlines offer even more attractive discounts.

El Al
(800) 223-6700
- 15 % off APEX fares

Finnair
(800) 950-5000
- 50 % off New York to Helsinki

Student Savings

The airlines have numerous programs that will provide savings for younger travelers. These special rates can be grouped into three general classes: children's fares, youth fares, and student fares. Age requirements vary by airline, but the general guideline is children are under age 12, youth are ages 14-24, and students are college students. Let's take a look at each of these opportunities for savings.

■ CHILDREN'S FARES

Children under 2 years of age are generally not required to have a seat, and can be carried by an adult over age 15. If the flight on which you are traveling is not full, your child may use an adjacent empty seat. One adult customer traveling with more than one infant must purchase an adjacent seat for each additional child, at the applicable child's fare. All additional children must be properly secured in their seats. Most airlines allow infants (under age 2) to occupy a reserved seat at half-fare as long as they are seated in a government approved safety seat.

Airlines very often have special rates for children age 2-11. These promotions vary from the popular *"Kids Fly Free"*, to special published fares for children. Some airlines offer special *"Family Saver Fares."* Check with the individual airlines. Here are some current programs:

Delta *Kids Fly Free*
800-221-1212
www.delta-air.com

- one child ages 2-11, per adult traveler, can fly free on flights between New York and Boston on weekends
- can be used for one-way flights

AccessAir *Family Saver Fares*
877-462-2237
www.accessair.com

- families flying with a member under age 26
- single traveler under age 26
- group of five or more traveling together
- New York/Los Angeles is $139 o/w—other options
- no advance purchase required

Sun Country Airlines *Kids Fares*
800-752-1218
www.suncountry.com

- one child ages 2-17, per adult traveler, can fly free on flights between Minneapolis/St. Paul and Orlando
- Minneapolis/St. Paul to East or West Coast is $99 one-way—other options are available

■YOUTH FARES

There are a limited number of possibilities for children in the youth age range, and they usually contain time restrictions. The best source of information on these options is *Best Fares* magazine (see the Print Resources chapter). Here are a few of the popular youth fare programs.

Martinair *Youth Perks*
800-627-8462
www.martinairusa.com

- open to travelers ages 12-26
- travel to Amsterdam
- for travel summer, 1999

Sabena *Swing Fares*
800-955-2000
www.sabena.com

- open to travelers ages 12-26
- travel to Europe
- for travel fall 1999

AirTran *X Fares*
800-247-8726
www.airtran.com

- open to travelers ages 12-26
- $45/segment travel to 31 U.S. cities
- no advance reservations
- no checked luggage
- standby only (best days are Tuesday and Wednesday).

Delta *Children Fare*
800-335-8218
www.delta-air.com

- program provides a 20% discount for children ages 2-12 traveling with their parents.

Air France *Youth and Student Pass*
800-237-2747
www.airfrance.fr

- LeFrance Youth and Student Pass is available for anyone under age 25, or students under age 27. The pass must be purchased in the U.S. and allows unlimited travel on Air France or Air Inter on any seven days in a 30-day period.

■ STUDENT FARES
Students ages 12-25 should investigate the Student Identity Card available from the non-profit Council on International Educational Exchange. You can receive their free catalogue at 800-226-8624. This card will give you access to many special student fares and is available for $15 per year.

TWA *Youth Travel Pak*
800-221-2000

www.twa.com

TWA's Youth Travel Pak is available to students ages 14-24, if you can provide a valid school ID. The Pak contains four coupons available for $548. Each coupon can be redeemed for a one-way ticket between cities in the Continental U.S. served by TWA. Travel to Hawaii requires two coupons for each segment. The Pak also contains a European Bonus Certificate redeemable for a 20% discount on a published fare to Europe. Usually reservations must be made at least 14 days in advance.

TWA *Student Getaway*
800-221-2000

www.twa.com

TWA's Student Getaway program is available to full time students ages 16-26. The program allows 10% off most domestic and international airfares. The discount card is $15 for one year and $25 for two years.

Campus Travel/Air France *European Hip Hop Airpass*
www.campustravel.co.uk

Here is an airpass for travelers under age 26 that provides a choice of 96 European cities. Hips are non-stop flights, and hops employ stopover cities during single day travel. Hips cost $87, while hops cost $129. Alitalia has a similar pass for use within Italy.

American Airlines *College SAAver*
wwwr1.aa.com

American Airlines provides discount airfares and travel specials exclusively for full-time students. You must sign up on-line for exclusive periodic e-mail updates.

British Airways *Britain on a Budget*
877-436-2081

www.budgetbritain.com.

British Airways has several holiday packages available to full-time students under age 35 and all travelers under age 26. Their London package starts at $649 for three nights and the Britain package starts at $769 for seven nights.

America West

americawest.com

800-235-9292

Students ages 17 through 25 traveling with America West can receive a ten-percent discount on published fares from the U.S. to Mexico.

■ OTHER OFFERS

Here are some additional opportunities for students to save on airfares.

American Airlines/Citibank *College Savings Certificates*

888-843-2484

www.citibank.com

Here's an opportunity to receive a no-fee Citibank Credit Card that comes with four domestic travel certificates, one domestic companion travel certificate, and three international travel certificates.

The four domestic travel certificates are each good for a discounted round-trip ticket worth from $139 - $299, valid on American Airlines and American Eagle flights originating within the contiguous 48 United States.

The Companion Travel Certificate lets you and a friend travel on the same trip for the same deal as the Domestic Travel Certificate.

The three International Travel Savings Certificates are good for savings of up to $250 off round-trip travel from the contiguous 48 United States to:

- Certificate 1: Europe or the United Kingdom
- Certificate 2: The Caribbean, Central America or South America
- Certificate 3: Mexico or Hawaii

United *College Plus*

www.collegeplus.com

United College Plus is a new frequent flyer program that allows students from any accredited university in the U.S. to earn miles toward free travel.

United College Plus is a student version of the United Airlines Mileage Plus frequent flyer program. Every time you fly a paid, qualifying flight on United or one of their partners, you'll not only earn "flight miles," you'll also earn special "bonuses."

Part-Time Travel Agent

In this section, I will describe some of the many ways to receive travel discounts and benefits by forming an affiliation with a travel agency.

■ REBATE AGENCIES

Rebate agencies are travel agencies that rebate (refund) part of their commission to travelers who make all of their own travel arrangements. After paying the fees on your tickets, the savings will usually range from 5-8 %.

Rebate agencies operate like airline consolidators, and are interested in high volume ticket sales. However, unlike consolidators, they sell cruises, tours, car rentals, and hotel reservations. The rebate agency buys large blocks of tickets at a huge markdown because of their volume discount.

Often the rebate agency is offering consolidator tickets, and your rebate is based on this already discounted price. While these agencies operate somewhat like travel clubs, they charge no membership fees.

If you would like to investigate the use of a rebate agency, here are two recently appearing on the Internet.

Pennsylvania Travel   800-331-0947

- Rebates usually amount to 10% of the ticket price with an additional fee based on your total expenditure.

Travel Avenue   800-333-3335

- Offers rebates of 5-12% on fares over $300. Their fees vary on a sliding scale determined by number of passengers.

Since they buy tickets in bulk and often use preferred providers, rebate agencies can frequently provide excellent ticket discounts. As with any discount strategy, it will pay to shop around.

■ EDUCATIONAL TOURS

Probably the easiest, quickest way to receive free travel is by organizing an educational tour. It is possible to receive a free ticket by signing up as few as six people for a tour package. This option is particularly attractive to teachers who enjoy several months of free time. In addition, they are also in a position to interest students in one of the many popular, reasonably priced tours. High school teachers are constantly solicited by the educational tour operators to participate in one of their programs.

While most of the participants in educational tours are high school students, about 25% of the travelers are adults looking for educational or academic rewards. If the teachers can sign up more students (beyond the six required for a free ticket), they receive additional compensation.

This travel opportunity is not limited to high school teachers. Parents and others interested in educational touring frequently take advantage of this strategy. It is often a natural for clergy or community workers who are usually working with area youngsters.

If you are interested in this type of tour there are several things to keep in mind.

- This is not luxury touring. Students will be willing to stay four-to-a-room, in a two star hotel, far from the city center. This type of accommodation may not meet your expectations.
- Most tour locations are selected to be of interest to high school students whose interests may not match yours.
- It would certainty help if you are comfortable being constantly surrounded by teenagers. Non-teachers are often unaware of the stress that may come with managing a group of teenagers on a daily basis.

Subsets of the educational tour businesses are the tours designed for college students. For the traveler whose main concern is travel cost benefits, this option is not as popular as the high school student tours. Tour packages for college students usually require the organizer to recruit *15* to *20* students before qualifying for one free ticket.

Another aspect of touring with college students involves destinations usually more suitable to partying. Many of these tours make no pretense of being "educational." Often the primary concerns of these packages are beer, beaches, and bikinis.

It is hard to find a better travel bargain than a free trip accompanied by a commission. If you would like to investigate the option of educational tours, here are several places to begin.

Educational Tours

CHA Educational Tours
215-923-7060

Cultural Heritage Alliance
215-923-7060

EF Educational Tours
800-637-8222

EF Educational Tours, Inc.
800-962-0060

Great Escape Tours
800-365-1833

College Tours

AESU Travel
800-638-7640

Gerber Tours, Inc.
800-645-9145

STA Travel
800-777-0112

Student Travel Services
800-648-4849

■ PACKAGE TOUR ORGANIZER

Here is another way to get free travel to the vacation destinations of your dreams. By organizing members of groups or clubs into a tour group, you can receive a free tour conductor pass. You will need to sign up 15 to 20 paying customers before you earn a free conductor pass. Your free pass will be for the land portion of the tour, and the airfare will remain your responsibility.

While the airlines refuse to deal with private individuals, more and more tour operators are willing to deal directly with the general public. You should be able to locate ads in popular travel magazines identifying travel wholesalers willing to book your tour.

Of course, you can always approach a local travel agent and negotiate a deal for your group. With the average tour price between $2,000-$3,000, a travel agent willing to kick back a portion of their commission would probably pay your airfare costs.

Several states have "travel provider laws" regulating the sale of any travel service. Be sure to check your state regulations before attempting to sell tour packages. Generally these laws do not pertain to an individual working through a travel agency as an "outside rep."

■ BUY A TRAVEL AGENCY

Of course, if you want to maximize your opportunity to receive the benefits of the travel industry (free trips and familiarization trips), you could simply buy an existing travel business. This is really not a viable option for the traveler simply looking for travel savings.

Purchase of an existing travel business would involve $50,000-$100,000 for the initial purchase, and additional costs of equipment, overhead, and staffing. If you have this kind of money available you're probably more concerned with a business opportunity, than a strategy to obtain an occasional free trip. Let's look at some other options.

■ GET A JOB AT A TRAVEL AGENCY

At first glance, it would appear that a job working at a travel agency might be the best of both worlds. On the one hand, you don't have the capital outlay of purchasing a travel business, and on the other hand, you are in position to locate travel bargains and receive travel industry benefits. Let's look a little closer at this option.

- Entry level salaries working at a small travel agency are very low. Many employees beginning salary ranges form $11,000-$13,000 per year, and the average travel agent's salary is about $15,000 per year.
- Agencies are usually looking for employees with at least 2 years of CRS (computer reservation system) experience.
- The work is usually pretty tedious. Most of your time will be spent doing paperwork or making reservations on the computer.
- You have very little time to actually travel. This is a 40-hour per week job with two weeks of vacation each year. Does this really sound like a job which will allow maximum use of travel benefits?

■ OUTSIDE SALES REPRESENTATIVE

While it is possible to sell travel as an individual, there are several reasons why you might want to consider a formal relationship with a travel agency.

- Airlines will only sell their tickets to agencies "accredited" with the proper industry organization. This means that unless you work with a travel agency accredited with ARC (Airline Reporting Corporation), you will be unable to purchase airline tickets for resale.
- Some states will not allow you to sell any travel services without special licenses and bonding.
- Travel agencies buy in bulk and form relationships with preferred wholesalers. In most cases, they will be able to buy travel packages cheaper than a private individual. As a result, they will probably sell these products at a lower price than a non-affiliated individual.
- A travel agency buying in bulk is more likely to receive special discounts and "fam" (familiarization trips).

- CRS (computer reservation system) access can be very costly. While it is possible to use easySABRE or Travelshopper, most Travel professionals use Apollo, or commercial Sabre, and these services can cost up to *$30* per hour to access.

What exactly is an outside sales representative? An outside representative is a person who brings business to a travel agency and receives commissions for that business. The "rep" receives no salary and for IRS tax purposes is not an employee of the travel agency, but is viewed as an "independent contractor." In other words, you have your own personal business (with whatever name you choose to call it), and are simply paid commissions on business you steer to a particular travel agency.

■ BIRD DOGS

A bird dog is a representative who simply steers business in the direction of a particular travel agency and lets the agency take it from there. It might involve family members, or it could be business associates. Since the bird dog simply brings in the business and does none of the planning or booking, are two types of outside representatives, commissions paid to the representative are usually 2-10% depending upon volume. If the bird dog is bringing substantial business to an agency, they might be rewarded with some free trips or special discounts, in addition to their commission.

■ TRADITIONAL OUTSIDE REPRESENTATIVES

Unlike the "bird dog", the traditional outside representative is involved with the actual planning and booking of the business delivered to the travel agency. The degree of involvement can vary from planning itineraries and researching prices to the actual booking on the agencies CRS. Usually the commission is based on the amount of work left to the travel agencies.

The outside representative is usually expected to do all the work except for the actual ticket creation. Some outside representatives have a CRS in their home along with their own ticket printers. Obviously these representatives require no additional work on behalf of the travel agency, and are rewarded by the highest levels of commission.

The outside representative who simply gets accounts to a travel agency with some basic planning of destinations and prices, will usually receive 10-20% of the commission. On the other hand, the rep that takes the client all the way through the booking process will receive 50-80% of the commission. The actual commission you receive is a matter of your negotiation with the travel agency.

■ LOCAL AGENCY

For many people, the most comfortable way to become an outside rep will be to develop an association with a local travel agency. There are several advantages to using this approach. If the agency is in your local area, it is both quick and convenient. If you need help, it is near at hand. The same is true if problems develop. Sometimes problems with an agency on the opposite coast are difficult to solve on the telephone.

There can also be some disadvantages to using a local agency. What if your local agency just isn't interested in using outside reps? It might be difficult to locate a local agency that is willing to have you work with them. Another possible disadvantage could be the local agency's size. A small local agency might pay a smaller commission split than you would prefer, and it might not qualify for as many travel benefits to share with an outside representative.

■ INSTANT AGENCY

Rather than form an alliance with a local travel agency, most people interested in becoming an outside rep choose one of the many travel agencies actively seeking the independent contractors. These agencies are viewed as "instant" agencies because once you pay your sign-up fees, you become an instant sales representative. Their procedures and policies vary widely. Most will accept people with little or no travel sales experience, however. They usually operate on a national basis, so your location is of no concern to them.

Forming an affiliation with an instant agency can have a number of advantages. It usually requires no previous travel experience and often the agency will provide significant training. However, agencies offering extensive training programs usually charge higher sign-up fees. If you shop around, you can probably find an agency willing to offer a better commission split than a local agency.

On the negative side, some of these (although not all) charge expensive sign-up fees. These fees vary from $49 to more than $6,000. Another possible source of problems is their location. It is very often difficult to solve problems over the telephone with a nameless employee several states distant from your location. The distance factor also makes it much more difficult to provide immediate services or tickets.

Instant agencies can be divided into three distinct types of organizations. Let's take a brief look at each of these types.

- Business Partnership—Agencies in this class appeal to those with significant past travel industry experience. They expect a pure business-to-business relationship, and are not interested in training inexperienced representatives. They usually have low sign-up fees, and typically pay higher commissions.

- Franchise Association—Much higher sign-up fees characterize the franchise operations. These agencies often require you to purchase hardware to become fully automated. They usually provide extensive training programs that enable the outside rep to become reasonably proficient using the CRS. These organizations most often appeal to travel industry neophytes.

- Card Mills—These operations are also known as referral agencies. Their sign-up fees are usually about $500, and their commission splits are often low. Their primary emphasis is to provide photo ID cards to people more interested in discount travel than the travel industry itself. Although these agencies are very controversial within the travel industry, they are very attractive to those interested in quickly obtaining travel benefits. In addition, these agencies often add an element of MLM (multi-level marketing) by offering you a percentage of the commission generated by those you recruit to their organization.

The International Airline Travel Agents Network (IATAN) is the Better Business Bureau of the travel business. Membership in this organization assures the public that they are dealing with "bona fide" travel professionals. They issue ID cards to employees of member travel agencies who sell ABOUT $4,000 worth of business each calendar year. While "card mills" will issue you their ID card, most travel suppliers only accept the IATAN card.

If you believe you might be interested in an affiliation as an outside representative, there are some critical questions that should be asked before you sign a contract with any travel agency. The correct answer, of course, depends upon whether your primary goal is to become a travel professional or just sell some travel as a means to subsidize your personal travel wishes and dreams.

■ QUESTIONS

- Is your agency accredited and in good standing with ARC and/or IATAN?
- How long has your agency been in business?
- What is your agency's gross sales volume?
- What sort of discounts or "fams" do you provide to outside agents? What is required to earn them?
- What commission splits does your organization offer?
- Do you require, or offer, any specialized training?
- What volume of sales is required to qualify for an IATAN card?
- What CRS do you use, and do you require outside agents to buy hardware or pay CRS access fees?
- Do you offer MLM opportunities as an inducement for recruiting additional agents?
- Do you offer IRS approved independent contractor status?
- How and when are commissions paid?
- Do you work through any preferred providers?
- Are any wholesalers or providers unavailable?
- Are there any annual fees required?
- What are your sign-up fees? Can they be paid in installments?

For anyone who is considering affiliation with an instant agency, it is essential that you understand the pros and cons of each type of organization. I urge you to read both of the following books *before* making any decisions.

PART-TIME TRAVEL AGENT:

HOW TO CASH IN ON THE EXCITING NEW WORLD OF TRAVEL MARKETING

Kelly Monoghan
1994 The Intrepid Travelers
$24.95

This volume is a complete business system with detailed instructions on setting up your own travel business.

A SHOPPERS GUIDE TO INDEPENDENT AGENT OPPORTUNITIES

Kelly Monaghan
1995 The Intrepid Traveler
$39.95

This book offers information about becoming an outside travel agent and the travel industry benefits that you can obtain. It contains information on agencies, sign-up fees, and commission splits to help you narrow your search. If you have plans to become a part-time travel agent, this book is indispensable.

Flexible Flyers

■ FLEXIBLE FLYER PLANS

Throughout this book I have repeatedly mentioned the benefits of being flexible. This strategy takes maximum advantage of that ability. There are two competing companies offering exceptional discounts for the flexible flyer. Although these companies are not highly advertised, they have served the college-backpacking crowd for years. The two companies are "Air-tech" and "Airhitch." Here is their proposition.

If you let them choose your exact date of departure, they will fly you at a substantial discount. If you are the type of person who can live with the uncertainty of these arrangements you can travel at terrific discounts. They have similar programs for Mexico and the Caribbean.

■ AIRHITCH

Airhitch is a company started by student travelers in the late sixties as a method to get back and forth across the Atlantic during vacation periods at a reasonable fare. In recent years the concept has been expanded to include travel to many other geographical regions of interest to both university students and to other travelers who insist on bargain airfares. Airhitch is based upon the concept of last minute seating availability on a "space available" basis. As with consolidator tickets, all travel takes place on regularly scheduled commercial aircraft.

Every day, thousands of seats are unsold on commercial flights. Airhitch allows the airlines to sell these seats at the last minute without endangering their fare structure. You travel in the seats next to passengers who have paid the standard full-fare.

To begin the process you call Airhitch and register. You specify the region you will be departing from and name three destination preferences. You will be asked to name a departure date with a "date range" of five days minimum duration. Shortly before your expected departure date, you call Airhitch and they will inform you of the expected flight opportunities and expected seat availability.

At this point you simply wait for the call giving you the final flight schedule. While no passenger using Airhitch is assured a precise destination on a specific date, in many cases you will arrive at your choice location. In any case, you will be in the specific general region and can use economical ground transportation to arrive at your ultimate destination.

One question that is often asked is, "Can two or more people use the service to travel together?" The answer is, "Yes." No one is ever obligated to board a flight, so if only one seat was available, you would simply wait for the next flight with enough available seats.

Most of the preceding information and procedures are specific to Airhitch-Europe. Another branch of the company called Airhitch-USA handles flights within the U.S. and to Hawaii. Yet another branch, Sunhitch® serves the resort destinations of Mexico and the Caribbean. Here are some samples of recent fares:

- East Coast/ Europe $159 o/w $318 r/t
- West Coast/ Europe $239 o/w $478 r/t
- Northeast/Florida $79 o/w $158 r/t
- West Coast/Hawaii $119 o/w $238 r/t

Here are some sample **Sunhitch** round-trips, based on a one-week stay at Mexican Resorts and the Caribbean Islands:
- Northeast to Mexico/ Caribbean $159
- California to Pacific Mexican Coast $189
- Midwest to Mexico/ Caribbean $209

Arrangements for travel with Airhitch or one of their associated services can be arranged using the Internet or by telephone.

Airhitch® International
New York 800-326-2009
Los Angeles 800-397-1098
San Francisco 800-834-9192
Paris 47.00.08.23
e-mail@http://www.airhitch.org/

■ AIR-TECH LTD

Air-tech is another company designed for the flexible flyer. Air-tech offers several plans from the space-available option to full first class service. They also offer a courier service for those with the ability to travel with only carry-on luggage.

Air-tech's most popular and economical program is called the FlightPass. The FlightPass program uses unsold seats on commercial airlines to provide economical, space-available, region-to-region travel.

You can call or e-mail Air-tech to begin the process. You will be asked to select a departure city and a preferred destination. You will then provide a two-four day travel window. Unlike Airhitch, the Air-tech FlightPass is for your preferred destination only. If the preferred destination is not available, you can choose to fly to another destination in the same region, or simply wait until your select location is available.

After Air-tech receives your order, your FlightPass is sent via Express Mail. Then simply call shortly before your travel window to receive information on the available flight options. At the airport you exchange your FlightPass for a boarding pass and you are on your way. On the odd chance that your flight sells out while you are at the airport, Air-tech will contact another carrier to provide another flight option. They claim to have a 94% success rate for their space-available customers.

Here are some sample Air-tech fares:

- Northeast/Europe $169 o/w
- Westcoast/Europe $229 o/w
- Northeast/Mexico $199 r/t
- Westcoast/ Mexico $239 r/t
- San Francisco/Honolulu $119 o/w
- Los Angeles/Maui $119 o/w

* o/w represents one-way travel; r/t represents a round-trip ticket.

To make arrangements with Air-tech contact:

Air-Tech Ltd.
212-219-7000
e-mail@ http://www.airtech.com/

Print Resources

In this section I have listed some books and newsletters you might find useful as you continue learning strategies to beat the airlines at their own game. While this list is by no means all-inclusive, it does give you a very select roster of the very best written on the subject of bargain airfares.

As I've mentioned repeatedly, knowledge corresponds to dollars saved, so I hope the information on these pages will save you hundreds of dollars on every future flight.

Books

A SHOPPERS GUIDE TO INDEPENDENT AGENT OPPORTUNITIES
Kelly Monaghan
1995 The Intrepid Traveler
$39.95

This book offers information about becoming an outside travel agent and the travel industry benefits that you can obtain. It contains information on agencies, sign-up fees, and commission spits to help you narrow your search. If you have plans to become a part-time travel agent, this book is indispensable.

AIR COURIER BARGAINS
HOW TO TRAVEL WORLD-WIDE FOR NEXT TO NOTHING
Kelly Monoghan
1996 The Intrepid Traveler
$14.95

Probably the definitive book on becoming an air courier. Kelly Monoghan provides a readable informative guide combined with an extensive listing of courier agencies.

AIRFARE SECRETS EXPOSED
THE HOW-TO RESOURCE GUIDE TO THE ABSOLUTE
LOWEST FARES ON THE MARKET
Sharon Tyler and Matthew Wunder
1994 Universal Information Corp. Publishing Co.
$16.95

This book covers consolidators, air couriers, charter flights, frequent flyer programs, and air pass programs. The book contains a valuable section on foreign entry requirements.

CONSOLIDATORS
AIR TRAVEL'S BARGAIN BASEMENT
Kelly Monoghan
1995 The Intrepid Traveler
$6.95

A comprehensive listing of airline consolidators with listings in Europe, Asia, Africa, South America, Australia and the Caribbean.

FLY FOR LESS 1996
Gary E. Schmidt
1996 Travel Publishing, Inc.
$19.95

This book provides information on over *180* consolidators and wholesalers along with ratings by travel agents and industry experts. It also provides complete corporate data and sales policies. The book is a shortened version of "The Index to Air Travel Consolidators" designed for the public rather than travel agents.

FLY THERE FOR LESS
HOW TO SAVE MONEY FLYING WORLDWIDE
Bob Martin
1990 Teak Wood Press
$8.95

The original book detailing the secrets of low-cost air travel. While this book is out-of-print it remains one of the very best treatments on the subject of ploys and strategies to obtain discount airfares. The major drawback of this book is a failure to provide adequate source listings.

PART-TIME TRAVEL AGENT:
HOW TO CASH IN ON THE EXCITING NEW WORLD OF TRAVEL MARKETING
Kelly Monoghan
1994 The Intrepid Travelers
$24.95

This volume is a complete business system with detailed instructions on setting up your own travel business.

INSIDER TRAVEL SECRETS
YOU'RE NOT SUPPOSED TO KNOW
Tom Parsons
1997 Best Fares USA, Inc.
$19.95

Probably the best travel reference book available. Parsons covers airlines, hotels, car rentals and cruises. He also includes hundreds of money saving tips. This volume is a total travel guide containing detailed references to just about every business providing travel or accommodation.

SMART TRAVEL
TOTAL PLANNING ON YOUR COMPUTER
1995 Ziff-Davis Press
$24.95

This book is a compilation by seven travel writers of information on using your computer to plan travel vacations. The book contains a CD-ROM (dos) to assist your planning. The usefulness of this book is probably limited due to the rapid explosion of information on the World Wide Web.

THE ART OF NO HASSLE DISCOUNT TRAVEL
Dave Huetten
1995 Basic Publishing

2307 114th Drive Northeast

Lake Stevens, WA 98258

A small book with many tips on airlines, cruise ships, car rentals, lodging, tours, and dining discounts.

THE COURIER AIR TRAVEL HANDBOOK
LEARN HOW TO TRAVEL WORLD WIDE FOR NEXT TO NOTHING
Mark I. Field

1994 Thunderbird Press, USA

$9.95

While not as readable as Kelly Monoghan's courier book, this volume does contain a valuable resources section. It also contains a listing of international hostels and bed and breakfast lodgings.

THE INDEX TO AIR TRAVEL CONSOLIDATORS
THE PROFESSIONAL GUIDE TO SELECTING CONSOLIDATORS AND WHOLESALERS
Gary E. Schmidt

1997 Travel Publishing, Inc.

$38.90

This volume created specifically for travel agents contains a comprehensive list of consolidators and wholesalers and includes ratings of each firm done by travel agents themselves. The book also provides corporate information, airline ticket information, booking procedures, and sales policies. It is an indispensable aid to the travel professional.

THE WORLDWIDE GUIDE TO CHEAP AIRFARES
HOW TO TRAVEL THE WORLD WITHOUT BREAKING THE BANK
Michael Wm. McColl

1995 Insider Publications

$14.95

This book covers the three best bargain airfare strategies — consolidators, charters and couriers. The format organized by hub cities in North America, Europe, Asia and Australia is somewhat cumbersome.

TICKETING PLOYS
BEATING THE AIRLINES AT THEIR OWN GAME
Kelly Monoghan
1995 The Intrepid Traveler
$4.00

A short report by Kelly Monoghan covering 7 specific tactics to obtain discount airline tickets.

1999 BEST TRAVEL DEALS
Consumer Reports
$8.95

This buying guide is distributed by the publishers of the *Consumer Reports Travel Letter*. The book has a small section titled airfare know-how containing some information on charters and consolidators.

FLY CHEAP
Kelly Monoghan
1999 The Intrepid Traveler
$14.95

This excellent book provides discussions of ticketing ploys, air passes, consolidators, and air couriers, and becoming a travel agent. There is a ton of good information here, and Kelly's style is witty and readable.

10 Minute Guide to
Travel Planning on the Net
Thomas Pack
1996 Que Corporation
$14.95

This guidebook for travel planning on the Internet will give you help with the essentials of booking online. The material is presented in a series of 10-minute lessons.

Magazines/Newsletters

THE AIRFARE REPORT
7709 Queen Avenue North
Minneapolis, MN 55444
(612) 569-9950

This newsletter is the most informative on the subject, and well worth the $65 yearly subscription rate. Your subscription fee actually buys you two separate monthly publications, *The Buyer's Guide to the Low Fare Airlines* and *The Consumer's Guide to the High Fare Airlines.*

INSIDE FLYER
4715-C Town Center Drive
Colorado Springs, CO 80916-4709
719-597-8880
www.insideflyer.com

If you are interested in the latest information on frequent flyer programs this is the monthly publication for you. A yearly subscription is $36.

THE SAVVY TRAVELER NEWSLETTER
1746 N Street, NW
Washington DC 20036
888-728-8728

Here is a monthly publication produced by radio host Rudy Maxa. It is full of travel tips and techniques. A yearly subscription is $49.

SENIOR AIRFARE BARGAIN REPORT
Jens Jurgen
Travel Companion Exchange
P.O. Box 833-S
Amityville, NY 11701-0833

Here is a source for up-to-date information on senior airfare coupon booklets. The report is $3.

Consumer Reports Travel Letter
Subscription Department
P.O. Box 51366
Boulder, CO 80323-1366
800-234-1970

Here is a great general travel newsletter. It often contains discount airfare information. Yearly subscriptions are $39.

BEST FARES
Discount Travel Magazine
P.O. Box 171212
Arlington, TX 76003
800-880-1234

The best discount magazine in the business. *Best Fares* is published monthly and a subscription includes passwords to their Internet site. A one-year subscription to *Best Fares* is $59.95.

PART III

Short Subjects

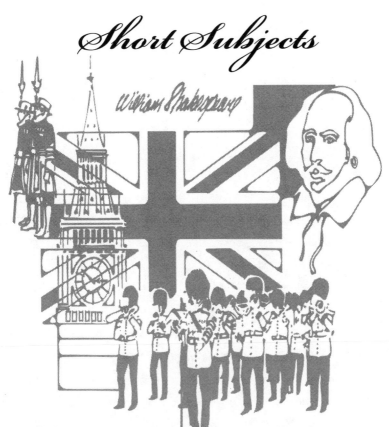

Part III of this guide will give you some additional techniques
that can often be piggybacked onto other strategies you have
already learned to provide you with the maximum possible
savings.

Short Subjects

■ NEW ROUTES

In the chapter on upstart airlines, I discussed how their introductory pricing often leads to great discounts. An existing airline opening a new route is another common possibility. In order to publicize their new route, and steal a few passengers, an airline will advertise a special introductory rate for travel on its new route. This price will usually only last for a specific period of time, but it can be heavily discounted. Airlines are constantly moving into new market areas in an attempt to pressure their competition, so always be alert to this possibility.

■ STRIKES AND BANKRUPTCIES

When an airline goes through a strike, all of its normal passengers are forced to choose another carrier. Once the strike is settled, the airline needs some incentive to win back their customers. The easiest and most common method employed is to offer fare discounts for a limited time.

In recent history, to recover after a strike, several domestic airlines have offered a special "comeback" fare with a $50^{\%}$ discount. These strike settlement fares may last a week or go on for as long as a month. Since they will be heavily advertised, you should be ready to take advantage of them when they are offered.

The same opportunities may be available after bankruptcy reorganization. When TWA went to bankruptcy court in the mid 90's, part of their reorganization plan required them to pay off Wall Street investor Carl Icon. Icon had earlier purchased the airline, and many felt drove it directly into bankruptcy court with his management style.

At the time of the bankruptcy hearings, the airline owed Icon nearly $200,000,000. As part of the reorganization, the court gave Icon the permission to purchase millions of dollars of TWA tickets at a major discount (rumored to be 50%). Icon then resold these tickets to the public at a smaller discount (25% on international TWA flights and 20% on TWA domestic flights). The single caveat was that these tickets be resold without advertising, simply by distributing them to a few selected travel agents.

It will take years for Icon to recover his losses, so as you read this book, these savings may still be available. The tickets were available by calling 800-497-6678. Sometimes it pays to watch the news.

This is a case where keeping current on news articles can help you locate discount airfares.

■ BACKHAULING
On a recent trip to Europe, my return flight from London to the U.S. had a stopover in Amsterdam. I boarded the flight at London's Heathrow Airport along with about 20 other passengers and the flight crew. This flight didn't appear on the airport departure listings, and is known in the business as a "backhaul." The primary purpose of the initial leg was to get a flight crew in position for the Amsterdam to U.S. flight. After a two-hour layover, I reboarded the same aircraft with the same flight crew for the return flight to the U.S.

Often a flight away from your destination for part of the trip can be used to increase savings. To locate these flights you will often need the assistance of a good travel agent.

■ CIRCLE TRIPS
If you would like to visit two cities on the same trip, but can't make them meet the "open-jaws" restrictions, ask about a "circle fare." A circle fare allows you to travel between three cities at a substantially reduced fare. These trips usually require a Saturday night stay; however, each airline has its own particular requirements.

■ STOPOVERS
Most airlines have a four-hour free stopover policy. Don't overlook the possibility of using this to your advantage if you only need a short visit or business meeting. Consider the following: I leave Seattle on a New York round-trip with a four-hour layover in

Chicago. I have a two-hour business meeting near the airport, and continue on to New York where I spend my vacation. My return trip is routed through St. Louis where I use the four-hour stopover to visit my parents who now make it their home. I meet a connecting flight back to Seattle. I've combined a vacation, a business meeting, and a family visit all into one SEA/NY round-trip ticket. I've also combined several of the book's other strategies to purchase the round-trip at 60% off full fare. Always combine strategies and use your imagination to maximize savings.

■ MIX AND MATCH

Sometimes when you are unable to find a discount fare to your destination, you can use two connecting flights from two different airlines to save on your fare. This strategy is often possible if one of the airlines has a special fare or is flying through one of its hubs.

■ CODE SHARING

Code sharing is a little-known airline practice that is seldom understood by the average passenger. Under code-sharing agreements, airlines sell seats on each other's flights as though they were their own. A passenger buying a ticket on airline A, actually completes part of the trip on airline B. The problem with this arrangement is the fact that airlines use it to fool travel agents CRS systems into believing these are flights on a single airline.

Airlines use code-sharing to circumvent the way the CRS lists flights. Non-stop flights are listed first on the CRS system, then flights on a single airline are listed, and the last listing is for connecting flights on different airlines. Given the facts that a single travel agent itinerary request can generate up to 20 CRS screens of information, and that travel agents seldom look beyond the first few screens to select a flight. There is a tremendous advantage to being listed as a single airline flight. In addition, the flight gets listed twice—once by each airline.

Very often you will purchase your ticket at a substantial discount by purchasing from nonallied carriers. Always ask your travel agent whether the flights you are booking are code-shares. If your intended flight is a code-share, have your travel agent check the price from each of the carriers involved. One of the partners may be charging up to 30% more than the other.

■ WAIVERS

While each airline has its own specific rules for passengers to qualify for the best promotional fares, they can sometimes be induced to grant a waiver of their regulations. If you hope to negotiate a waiver, speak with a supervisor, but don't attempt to do it at a busy ticket window. Make it easy for the supervisor to grant the waiver by being discreet and using whatever documentation you need to state your circumstances. Be polite, and don't carry on the conversation in front of other passengers. Often it is possible to have your travel agent apply for the waiver when seeking your ticket.

Some of the more common waivers have been granted for medical emergencies, a death in your family, or a change in your trip itinerary. Always try to get a waiver on less popular or less crowded flights, such as, a "red eye". If one airline won't grant you a waiver, try another. By being persuasive, you might just get the waiver and save 20%-40% off full fare.

■ CLASSIFIED ADS

Don't overlook the possibility of finding some real airfare bargains in the local newspaper. Some of the best bargains on domestic airfares are found in the classified advertising section of any large metropolitan newspaper. Often this is the only practical way for someone to recover money on non-refundable tickets they are unable to use themselves. You may also locate some one-way tickets left over as a result of a creative traveler using some special technique mentioned elsewhere in this book.

As is usually the case when looking for bargains, you're going to have to be flexible. These tickets probably aren't going to go to the exact destination you prefer. The idea here is to use the airfare to get as close as possible, and use surface transportation on the final leg. Let's say you want to get to New York City, but the full fare is $500. You find tickets in the classified for $150 to Washington DC. Is it worth the extra $350 to take a bus or the shuttle to New York? These are questions that only you and your budget can answer.

To locate these tickets, look in the classified section, usually under the typical heading of "Tickets" or "Travel." Always check the Sunday edition, since this is the most popular edition for advertisements. Sunday editions will usually have a travel supplement, so don't overlook checking there to get a good bargain base rate.

In these times of greater airport security, there are several things to keep in mind if you purchase tickets from the classified section. First, you are purchasing from a total stranger, so verify with the airline that the ticket is valid. Secondly, remember the price you pay is negotiable, so the closer the departure date, the lower the ticket value. Finally, and probably most importantly, you will be using the name printed on the ticket to fly. It should at least be the proper gender, or security may detain you. John Doe may run into some difficulty using a ticket issued to Mary Smith.

■ CURRENCY FLUCTUATIONS

It is possible to use the fluctuation in the exchange rate between countries to achieve bargains with international airfares. The value of each country's currency is constantly changing in relation to the U.S. dollar. Some impressive savings can be gained by taking advantage of this fact. Most airfares are based on the currency of the country where the flight originates. A flight out of Los Angeles will be based on dollars, while a flight out of Paris will be based on Francs. If you live in LA and purchase a Paris/LA round-trip ticket, the price will be in francs because Paris is the originating city of your flight.

For some very specific ways to use currency fluctuations to your advantage check the section on "Round Robins" which follows.

■ ROUND ROBINS

Round Robins are an especially sweet strategy for business travelers. Their savings are dependent upon the currency fluctuations mentioned in an earlier chapter. If you are a business traveler and travel to Europe four times each year, you begin this strategy by finding the cheapest one-way ticket to Europe. Using a strategy like "Air-Hitch," you can probably get there for $100-$150. Now you begin to use the "Round Robin" strategy.

In addition to currency fluctuations, flights originating in Europe to the U.S. are traditionally 10%-15% cheaper than if the flights originate in the U.S. Use this to your advantage. Buy a round-trip ticket to the U.S. and have the travel agent or consolidator leave an open date on the return portion of the ticket. When you make your next trip to Europe use the return portion of the ticket to get there. When you are ready to return from Europe buy your ticket there and repeat the process.

Currency fluctuations, airfare prices, and convenience will guide you in locating your best buy in Europe (London, Paris, or Amsterdam). London is famous for their "bucket shops" with outstanding airfare bargains. Many U.S. businesses have been using this strategy with their employees for years. Why not take advantage of it simply as a bargain-conscious traveler?

■ ONE-WAY

Sometimes I am asked if there is any possible way to save on one-way tickets. Airlines usually price their one-way tickets higher than a round trip full fare promotional ticket. The solution here is to buy the round trip promotional fare and throw away, or resell the return coupon.

For example, I am taking a trip with friends to New York by automobile and would like to return to Seattle by air. A New York /Seattle one way ticket is $890. I can buy a Seattle /New York round-trip promotional fare for $296. I go for the round-trip ticket, but I purchase a New York to Seattle round trip, so that the ticket I use is always the top coupon.

If I were to purchase a Seattle-New York round-trip, I wouldn't be using the top coupon and the airline computer system would cancel my New York-Seattle return assuming I had not made the trip. Always plan ahead if you only plan to use a portion of your ticket.

■ TRAVEL CLUBS

Travel clubs began as organizations offering special services and discounts to automotive travelers. Recently they have expanded their services to include hotel discounts, dining discounts, car rental discounts, package tour and cruise discounts, and airfare discounts.

A recent *Consumer Reports* article showed that just about any of the discount airfare strategies described in this book will beat the reduced airfare packages offered to travel club members, without the required annual dues. If you are interested in comparing travel clubs, go to the library and obtain the October 1995 issue of *Consumer Reports.*

■ ODD DAYS, RED EYES, AND STANDBY

Just as there are certain days when the airlines are jammed and crowded, there are days and times when the airlines struggle to fill their available seats. How many people do you think are looking for an all day flight on Thanksgiving Day?

The "red eye" (midnight to 4-am departure) flights are almost always considerably cheaper to book. Sometimes unannounced special early morning fares are placed in the airline reservation computers to spur sales on a particular route, so don't overlook calling the reservation system at 3 AM to check on a fare. The special fare might go into the computer system at midnight and be over by 6 AM. It doesn't happen every day, but real bargains always take a little extra investigation. Always be willing to fly standby. If you are flexible, standby can lead to some great bargains.

Why not combine standby with a red-eye flight on an odd day? You will probably get a real bargain price, and the odds of not making your expected flight go way down. Standby booking also has another advantage that you should investigate. Standby fares are most common on international flights, and since they are not part of any promotional pricing, often they can be purchased one-way. The idea here would be to check exchange rate of the destination country. It's possible that two one-way standby tickets could save you up to 50% over the full round-trip fare.

■ PROMOTIONAL FARES

I have already mentioned APEX Promotional Fares on international flights, but the competition among domestic airlines has led to a variety of domestic promotional fares. These flights are marketed under names like "Super Saver" or "Ultra Saver." These promotional fares can be up to 50% less than full fares, so don't overlook them. Promotional fares are usually created by an airline's desire to expand into a new area, or to a new destination. These tickets will often carry additional restrictions, so make sure you know what you are purchasing.

■ COUPONS

Some globetrotting travelers have accumulated frequent flyer certificates that they would rather sell than use personally. Others have collected "bump" coupons they might want to sell rather than use. These travelers might sell their coupons to a broker who, in turn, offers them to the public at a substantial saving over a full fare. You can locate these coupon brokers in the business or travel section of any major newspaper.

Buying coupons is, at best, a risky proposition, since exchanging coupons violates most airline rules. The practice, however, is not illegal and can lead to substantial savings, so I have chosen to mention it in this book. If you choose to employ this strategy be aware of the following precautions:

- Be aware of which airlines will overlook the practice violating their rules. There are several.
- Always make sure the broker reissues the ticket in your name.
- Make sure you check the expiration date before you buy.
- Make sure the broker will refund your money if the airline refuses to honor your coupon or confiscates it.
- Never let airline personnel know how you purchased the ticket.
- Always use a credit card.

■ TRAVEL AGENT

I assume that by this time you have come to the realization that an energetic, knowledgeable, and trusted travel agent should be able to employ most of the strategies you have learned in this book. If you are determined to always get a bargain on your airline tickets, you should probably spend some time cultivating a personal relationship with a professional travel agent.

Always explain the methods you would like the agent to employ, and let them know you understand that they are working on a commission. Your travel agent usually will work to get you some real airfare bargains if they realize they will be receiving substantial commissions on your cruise, tour, or hotel bookings. Cruise and tour commissions, in particular, are usually much more lucrative than the eight percent commission typically paid to small travel agencies for an airfare reservation.

Be selective in picking out the agency you want to work for you. Try out several agencies before making a decision. Try to spend at least as much time selecting a travel agent, as you were willing to devote to your search for a bargain airfare. The time you dedicate to making the best choice for a personal agent will save you considerable time and money later.

When you find an agency that consistently finds travel bargains for you, give them all your business. Let them know that you are recommending them to all your friends.

After choosing the agency with which you will be working, try to work with the same agent each time you place an order. Once the agent realizes you are always using them for your travel plans, you are on your way to developing the one-to-one relationship you seek.

Closing Tips

Well, there you have it. We've covered most of the territory and now it's up to you to decide. Using a consolidator is a bit of an adventure, but isn't that what puts a little spice into our lives anyway? If you're a conservative, "status quo" type, who would rather have your money in a bank account than invested in the stock market, a flight consolidator may not be your "cup of tea." You would probably be better served by a trusted travel agent. If you believe that you can use your imagination and creativity to maximize savings on your trip, then "go for it." Use your knowledge and imagination to plan strategies that will make your trip an adventure, and at the same time reward yourself with some great savings.

Always know what you're purchasing. Understand the airlines' policies and restrictions, such as length of stay and days of departure. Before you purchase tickets, check to see if they are non-transferable or non-refundable. Find out if you qualify for frequent flyer mileage, and remember to purchase your tickets with a credit card.

Whenever possible, find a way to use "hub" cities. Hub cities like San Francisco and New York have more airlines competing for passengers, and as a result, provide more opportunities for savings.

Always attempt to locate tickets that can be refunded or exchanged should your plans change at the last minute. Be sure to check on the minimum stay requirements. If your trip is planned to include an exceptionally long stay, or if you only need a one-way ticket, a consolidator is "made to order." In cases of emergencies or just last minute whims, consolidators are the only way to go. Happy traveling!

Appendixes

Appendix A

Travel Agent Consolidators

Appendix B

Airline Phone Numbers

Appendix A

Here is a list of consolidators who only work through travel agents.

Travel Agent Consolidators

Company Name	Phone	City	State
Abratours	800-227-2887	White Plains	NY
Agents Advantage	800-816-2211	Elizabeth	NJ
Air Tickets	800-207-7300	New York	NY
Airfax Airline Mrktg Assoc., Inc.	404-662-0885	Duluth	GA
Airplan, Inc.	800-866-7526	Pittsburgh	PA
Alta Tours	800-338-4191	San Francisco	CA
American Intl. Consolidators	800-888-5774	Elmsford	NY
American Travel Abroad Inc.	800-228-0877	New York	NY
Anderson International Travel	800-365-1929	East Lansing	MI
APC/American Passenger Cns	800-526-2447	New York	NY
Ariel Tours, Inc.	800-262-1818	Brooklyn	NY
ATC Travel	800-872-4601	Kissimmee	FL
Avanti Tourism	800-422-4256	Portland	OR
Balair/CTA	800-322-5247	New York	NY
Balkan Holidays	800-822-1106	New York	NY

Brazilian Travel Services	800-342-5746	New York	NY
Brendan Air	800-491-9633	Van Nuys	CA
C&H International	213-387-2288	Los Angeles	CA
C.L. Thompson Express	800-833-4258	Los Angeles	CA
C.L. Thompson Express	800-833-4258	New York	NY
Central Holidays	800-965-5000	Jersey City	NJ
Central Holidays	800-965-5000	Los Angeles	CA
Centrav, Inc.	800-874-2033	Minneapolis	MN
Charterways	800-869-2344	San Jose	CA
City Tours	800-238-2489	E. Rutherford	NJ
Classical Vacations	800-950-8654	Houston	TX
Consolidated Tours, Inc.	212-586-5230	New York	NY
Cosmopolitan TVC Ctr	800-548-7206	Ft. Lauderdale	FL
Creative Marketing Management	800-458-6663	New York	NY
CTI Carriers	800-363-8181	Toronto	ON
D-FW Tours	800-527-2589	Dallas	TX
Delights Travel	604-876-8278	Vancouver	BC
DER Tours Inc.	800-782-2424	Los Angeles	CA
Diplomat Tours	800-727-8687	Sacramento	CA
Eastern European Travel Center	718-339-1100	Brooklyn	NY
Embassy Tours-Latin America	800-299-5284	Dallas	TX
Europak Scan Divisions	800-253-1342	Baltimore	MD

Express Discount Travel	800-266-8669	San Diego	CA
Fantasiques Tours	310-577-6711	Marina del Rey	CA
Fantasy Holidays	800-645-2555	Jericho	NY
Fare Deals Travel	800-878-2929	Englewood	CO
Festival of Asia	800-533-9953	San Francisco	CA
Fourth Dimension Tours	800-343-0020	Miami	FL
G.G. Tours	416-487-1146	Toronto	ON
Gate 1	800-682-3333	Glenside	PA
Gateway Express Ltd.	800-334-1188	Portland	OR
Global Travel Consolidators	800-366-3544	Santa Monica	CA
Global Travel Network	800-366-3544	Santa Monica	CA
Go Way Travel	800-387-8850	Culver City	CA
Golden Pacific #1 Travel	800-500-8021	Brandon	FL
Golden Pacific Travel World	800-881-8881	Brandon	FL
Guardian Travel Service Ltd.	800-741-3050	St. Petersburg Bch.	FL
Hamilton, Miller	800-669-4466	Southfield	MI
Happy Tours	800-877-5262	Scotts Valley	CA
Holiday Travel International	800-775-7111	North Huntington	PA
HTI Tours	800-441-4411	Philadelphia	PA
Hungarian Travel, Inc.	800-624-9277	Reseda	CA
Intra Aussie Tours	800-531-9222	Los Angeles	CA
Intervac	800-992-9629	Miami	FL

ITS Tours & Travel	800-533-8688	College Station	TX
J & O Air	800-877-8111	San Diego	CA
Jade Tours	604-689-5885	Vancouver	BC
Jetset Tours Inc.	800-638-3273	Los Angeles	CA
Jetset tours Inc.	800-638-3273	Los Angeles	CA
Jetset Tours Inc.	800-638-3273	San Francisco	CA
Jetset Tours Inc.	800-638-3273	Chicago	IL
Jetset Tours Inc.	800-638-3273	New York	NY
Jetset Tours Inc.	800-638-3273	Houston	TX
Jetset Tours Inc.	800-638-3273	Seattle	WA
Leisure Resources	800-729-9051	Milford	CT
M & H Travel Inc.	800-356-9648	New York	NY
Marnella Tours Inc.	800-937-6999	Huntington Station	NY
MLT Vacations	800-328-0025	Minnetonka	MN
M T & T	612-784-3226	Minneapolis	MN
New Europe Holidays	800-642-3874	New York	NY
Northwest World Vacati	800-727-1111	Minnetonka	MN
Orbis Polish Travel, Inc.	800-876-7247	New York	NY
Orient Pacific Tours	800-663-0588	Vancouver	BC
Overseas Express	800-343-4873	Chicago	IL
Oxford Travel	800-851-5290	Beacon	NY
P & F International Inc.	800-822-3063	Brooklyn	NY
Pacific Gateway Inc.	800-777-8369	Portland	OR
Pacific Gateway	800-777-8369	Seattle	WA

Panorama Trs/Jensen Baron Trvl	800-527-4888	Salt Lake City	UT
Park Place International (PTS)	213-526-0933	Los Angeles	CA
Park South Travel	212-686-5350	New York	NY
Passport Travel Mgmt Group	800-950-5864	Tampa	FL
PCS-Atlanta, GA	800-832-6525	Atlanta	GA
PCS-Los Angeles	800-367-8833	Los Angeles	CA
Pleasure Break Vacations, Inc.	800-777-1566	Rolling Meadows	IL
Plus Ultra Tours	800-367-7724	New York	NY
Prime Travel Services, Inc.	800-447-4013	Coral Gables	FL
Queue Travel, Inc.	800-356-4871	San Diego	CA
Rahim Tours	800-556-5305	Lake Worth	FL
Rebel	800-227-3235	Valencia	CA
Rebel	800-732-3588	Orlando	FL
Skylink Travel	800-247-6659	New York	NY
Solar Tours	800-388-7652	Washington	DC
South Star Tours	310-436-1001	El Segundo	CA
STA Travel(Student Travel Ntwk)	800-825-3001	Boston	MA
STA Travel	800-825-3001	11 Locations in the U.S.	MA
STT Worldwide Travel	800-348-0886	Los Angeles	CA
STT Worldwide Travel, Inc.	800-348-0886	Beaverton	OR

Sun Makers	800-841-4321	Seattle	WA
Sunbeam Travel	800-247-6659	Los Angeles	CA
Sunbeam Travel	800-247-6659	Chicago	IL
Sunbeam Travel	800-247-6659	New York	NY
Sunbird	800-800-0202	San Jose	CA
Sunny Land Tours	800-783-7839	Hackensack	NJ
Sunrise Tours	800-872-3801	New York	NY
Surinam Airways	800-327-6864	Miami	FL
TFI Tours Intl. Ltd.	800-745-8000	New York	NY
Africa Desk, The	800-284-8796	New Milford	CT
Egyptian Connection, The	800-334-4477	Fresh Meadows	NY
Travel Group, The	800-836-6269	San Antonio	TX
Time Travel	800-847-7026	Bensenville	IL
TMV Tours	800-496-1285	Jersey City	NJ
Tours International Inc.	800-247-7965	Houston	TX
Trans Am Travel	800-822-7600	Alexandria	VA
Travel Beyond	800-823-6063	Wayzata	MN
Travel Express	800-333-3611	Salt Lake City	UT
Travel Leaders International	800-323-3218	Coral Gables	FL
Travel N Tours	800-854-5400	Beacon	NY
Travel Wholesalers	800-487-8944	Fairfax	VA
Travelogue, Inc.	800-542-9446	Greensboro	NC
Travnet Inc.	800-359-6388	Chicago	IL

Trek Holidays	800-661-7265	Edmonton	AB
TT Travel	800-685-0393	Seattle	WA
Unipac Viajes	800-892-2586	Portland	OR
United Tours Corp.	800-245-0203	New York	NY
Unitravel	800-325-2222	St. Louis	MO
Vacation-land	800-245-0050	San Francisco	CA
World Travel & Tours, Inc.	800-886-4988	Baileys Crossroads	VA
Worldvision Travel Services	800-545-7118	W. Orange	NJ
Wright Travel Holidays	800-877-3240	Turnersville	NJ
Ya'lla Tours	800-644-1595	Portland	OR

Appendix B

Airlines' Phone Numbers

Company Name	Reservations Phone
Aer Lingus	(800) 223-6537
Aero California	(800) 237-6225
Aerolineas Argentinas	(800) 333-0276
Aeromexico	(800) 237-6639
Aeroperu	(800) 777-7717
Air Canada	(800) 869-9000
Air France	(800) 237-2747
Air India	(800) 223-7776
Air Inter Europe	(800) 237-2747
Air Jamaica	(800) 523-5585
Air Malta	(800) 756-2582
Air Mauritius	(800) 537-1182
Air New Zealand	(800) 262-1234
Air Niugini	(714) 752-5440
Air Pacific	(310) 417-2236
Air Paraguay - LAPSA	(800) 677-7771
Air Wisconsin - UA Express	(800) 241-6522

Air Zimbabwe	(800) 228-9485
Airport Express	(800) 301-7275
Alaska Airlines	(800) 426-0333
Alitalia Airlines	(800) 223-5730
ALM Antillean Airlines	(800) 327-7230
Aloha Airlines	(800) 367-5250
America West Airlines	(800) 235-9292
American Airlines	(800) 433-7300
Ansett Australia Airlines	(800) 366-1300
APA International Air	(800) 693-0007
Asiana Airlines	(800) 227-4262
Austrian Airlines	(800) 843-0002
Avensa Airlines Inc.	(800) 428-3672
Avianca Airlines	(800) 284-2622
British Airways	(800) 247-9297
British Midland	(800) 788-0555
BWIA International Airways	(800) 538-2942
Canadian Airlines International	(800)-426-7000
Carnival Airlines	(800) 824-7386
Cayman Airways	(800) 422-9626
Continental Airlines	(800) 525-0280
Czech Airlines	(212) 765-6022

Delta Air Lines	(800) 221-1212
Eagle Canyon Airlines	(800) 446-4584
Eastern Australia Airlines	(002) 693-1000
Egyptair	(800) 334-6787
EL AL Israel Airlines	(800) 223-6700
Emirates Airlines	(800) 777-3999
Ethiopian Airlines	(800) 445-2733
Faucett Airlines	(800) 338-9691
Finnair	(800) 950-5000
Garuda Indonesia	(800) 342-7832
Hawaiian Airlines, Inc.	(800) 367-5320
Horizon Air	(800) 547-9308
Iberia Airlines of Spain	(800) 772-4642
Icelandair	(800) 223-5500
Japan Air Lines	(800) 525-3663
Kendell Airlines	(616) 921-5011
Kenya Airways	(800) 343-2506
Kiwi International Airlines	(800) 538-5494
KLM Royal Dutch Airlines	(800) 374-7747
LACSA	(800) 225-2272
Ladeco Chilean Airlines	(800) 825-2332
Lan Chile Airlines	(800) 735-5526

LOT Polish Airlines	(800) 223-0593
LTU International Airlines	(800) 888-0200
Malev Hungarian Airlines	(800) 223-6884
Martinair Holland	(800) 627-8462
Mexicana Airlines	(800) 531-7921
Middle East Airlines	(212) 664-7310
Midwest Express Airlines	(800) 452-2022
Nigeria Airways	(212) 935-2701
Northwest Airlines	(800) 225-2525
Olympic Airways	(800) 223-1226
Philippine Airlines	(800) 435-9725
Qantas Airways	(800) 227-4500
Royal Air Maroc	(800) 344-6726
Royal Jordanian	(800) 223-0470
Sabena Belgian World Airlines	(800)-955-2000
Saudi Arabian Airlines	(800) 472-8342
Scandinavian Airlines System	(800) 221-2350
Scenic Airlines	(800) 634-6801
South African Airways	(800) 722-9675
Swissair	(800) 221-4750
Tap-Air Portugal	(800) 221-7370
Trans Continental Airlines, AU	(613)-335-3522

Trans Jamaican Airline	(809) 929-0834
Trans World Airlines	(800) 221-2000
Transbrazil Airlines	(800) 872-3151
Turkish Airlines	(800) 874-8875
United Airlines	(800) 241-6522
USAir Inc	(800) 428-4322
Varig Brazilian Airlines	(800) 468-2744
Viasa-Venezuelan Int'l Airways	(305)-374-5000
Virgin Atlantic Airways	(800) 862-8621
World Airways	(800) 967-5350

Index

A

B

C

Happy Traveling

George E. Hobart